Tribute to Religion

The Grand Tour

Tribute to Religion

Flavio Conti

Translated by Patrick Creagh

HBJ Press
a subsidiary of Harcourt Brace Jovanovich, Inc.
New York

HBJ Press

President, Robert J. George
Publisher, Giles Kemp
Vice President, Richard S. Perkins, Jr.
Managing Director, Valerie S. Hopkins
Executive Editor, Marcia Heath
Series Editor, Carolyn Hall
Staff Editor, Chris Heath
Text Editors: Ernest Kohlmetz, Anne Mendelson, Joyce Milton
Editorial Production: Karen E. English, Ann McGrath, Eric Brus, Betsie Brownell, Patricia Leal, Pamela George
Project Coordinator, Linda S. Behrens
Business Manager, Richard White
Marketing Director, John R. Whitman
Public Relations, Janet Schotta
Business Staff: Pamela Herlich, Joan Kenney

Architectural Consultant, Dennis J. DeWitt
Text Consultant, Janet Adams
Design Implementation, Designworks

Rizzoli Editore

Authors of the Italian Edition: Dr. Flavio Conti, Paolo Favole, Giuliana Gattoni, G. M. Tabarelli
Idea and Realization, Harry C. Lindinger
General Supervisor, Luigi U. Re
Graphic Designer, Gerry Valsecchi
Coordinator, Vilma Maggioni

Photography Credits:

Carrese: p. 13 top and center, p. 19 top, p. 22, p. 23 bottom / *Cauchetier:* pp. 41–52 / *Dilia-Neubert:* p. 57, p. 58 bottom, p. 59, p. 60 bottom, p. 61, p. 68 / *Ferrari:* p. 9 / *Hassmann:* pp. 73–96, p. 108 bottom, pp. 109–115 / *Klammet & Aberl:* pp. 106–107 / *Maggioni:* p. 20 center left / *Magnum-Barbey:* p. 16 bottom, p. 17 bottom, p. 18 top, p. 32 / *Magnum-Gilles:* p. 137, pp. 140–147 / *Magnum-Hartmann:* p. 12 top, p. 21 / *Magnum-Lessing:* p. 58 top and center, p. 60 top right and center left and right, p. 62 top left, bottom left, and right, p. 64 top left and right, p. 65, p. 66 top and bottom left, p. 67, p. 105, p. 108 top, p. 116 / *Mauritius:* pp. 138–139, p. 148 / *Meuthonnen:* pp. 154–155 / *Publiaerphoto:* pp. 10–11 / *Radnicky:* p. 60 top left, p. 63 top and bottom, p. 64 center and bottom left, p. 66 bottom right / *Scala:* p. 12 bottom, p. 13 bottom, pp. 14–15, p. 16 top, p. 17 top, p. 18 bottom, p. 19 bottom, p. 20 top left and right and bottom left and right, p. 23 top, pp. 24–31 / *Stierlin:* p. 121, pp. 122–123, p. 124 top, pp. 125–128, p. 129 top left and right, p. 129 center left and bottom right, p. 131 top right, p. 132, p. 153, pp. 156–164 / *Widmer:* p. 124 bottom, p. 130, p. 131 top left, center, and bottom right.

Library of Congress Catalog Card Number: 78–61757
ISBN: 0–15–003735–X

Printed in Italy

Editorial Supervisor, Gianfranco Malafarina
Research Organizer, Germano Facetti
U.S. Edition Coordinator, Natalie Danesi Murray

Contents

Preface

Tribute to Religion

Architectural history, students have been known to sigh, is nothing but churches, churches, and more churches. Their protest is quite accurate. The history of architecture is composed for the most part of religious buildings—churches and temples, synagogues and mosques, stupas and ziggurats, pyramids and pagodas.

Ever since recorded history, people have expended vast amounts of energy and resources and devoted their highest abilities to building the shrines of their faith. The creation of religious buildings is, first and foremost, an act of homage to the deity—an imitation of the god's own work. Moreover, every civilization is naturally convinced that its gods are the greatest—indeed the only—ones, therefore deserving of the most magnificent temples. Undoubtedly, there is also sometimes a political reason for building monumental religious shrines. Kings have always considered themselves god's representatives on earth, and in the past the name of god was invoked to justify political and martial policies, however secular or arbitrary they really were.

The ancient Old-New Synagogue of Prague is both something less—and something more—than a national shrine. It commemorates the faith of a race and a culture—humble, even afraid at times, but ineradicable. The smallest, plainest, and most modest of religious buildings, Old-New is also touchingly venerable. According to legend, its stones were brought from Solomon's Temple of Jerusalem, and for 700 years the synagogue has been the flame burning at the center of the Jewish ghetto in Prague. Its stones have been sanctified by the blood of the faithful, martyred in many pogroms. Today the walls are inscribed with the names of thousands of Czechoslovakian Jews murdered by the Nazis. Ten thousand tombstones huddle in the tiny Jewish cemetery, a mute and enduring record of centuries of Jewish history.

Both the Old-New Synagogue of Prague and the Cathedral of Notre Dame are Gothic in style. But there the resemblance ends. On the banks of the Moldava a persecuted but tenacious people built the tabernacle of their faith; on an island in the Seine a royal house consecrated its dominion in stone. A foreigner who knows Paris only from postcards might make the mistake of imagining that the Eiffel Tower is the symbol of the nation. But no Frenchman would agree. Though the great church of the French kings was stormed to the tune of "La Marseillaise" during the Revolution, it has since become a sort of Marseillaise among monuments. One of the foreigners who overlooked its importance was Adolf Hitler. He did not see that a flame had been lit before the Madonna in Notre Dame on the day of the French surrender—a flame which continued to burn there day and night until, after four years of silence, the mighty bell of the cathedral rang out to tell the world that Paris was free again.

Notre Dame survived the war as a prisoner; Cologne Cathedral also escaped virtually intact. Although the Allies conducted a concentrated bombing campaign against this strategically important German city, leveling buildings all around the church, they succeeded in sparing the cathedral. The necessary restoration work was completed on August 15, 1948, in time to celebrate the seventh centenary of the laying of the cornerstone.

Cologne Cathedral, begun in 1248, is the largest Gothic cathedral in Northern Europe. It took 638 years to complete—the piety and funds of the Germany of Bismarck's time completed what the medieval bishops had begun. A landmark and symbol of the city, its spiky profile even graces the invitations to the annual Cologne furniture fair.

The temple of Angkor Wat in Cambodia also appears to have survived a war without irreparable damage. Photographs reaching the West in the last few years show the temple in much the same state of repair as before the Cambodian civil war.

Angkor Wat is probably the largest religious structure in the world. This temple-mountain, built by the Khmer King Suryavarman II in the twelfth century A.D. and dedicated to Vishnu, the "world preserver," represents the height of classical Khmer art. The most remarkable feature of the temple compound is its sculptural ornament, covering thousands of feet of wall with delicate low relief. The temple was abandoned in the fifteenth century and lay forgotten and overgrown with jungle vegetation until the mid-nineteenth century, when it was rediscovered by the French and restored as far as possible to its former glory.

The magnificent basilica of Hagia Sophia in Istanbul has also outlasted countless vicissitudes. Built under the Roman Emperor Justinian by Anthemius of Tralles and Isidorus of Miletus in the sixth century, Hagia Sophia is the supreme masterpiece of Byzantine architecture. Its floors, walls, and columns are of gleaming marble. Hagia Sophia's supreme triumph, however, is the massive golden dome. A seemingly miraculous light enters through the ring of windows in the base of the dome, flooding the interior and making the dome itself appear to hover weightlessly.

The Byzantine Empire was plundered by the Crusaders and felled by the Ottoman Turks in 1453, but the Moslems spared the Christian basilica, converting it to a mosque. Four minarets were added, and the brilliant figure mosaics were obscured under coats of whitewash. In the twentieth century, Hagia Sophia was transformed once again, when it became a museum of Byzantine art. Many of the mosaics, which date from the ninth century, have been cleaned and restored, and the basilica is now open to all regardless of creed.

Some conquerors have been less respectful than the Ottomans of the monuments which came into their possession. When, in 1533, Francisco Pizarro and his small band of Spaniards took the Incan capital of Cuzco, high in the mountains of southern Peru, they showed no mercy for native buildings or traditions. The Lord Inca was executed, and the Incas were baptized as Christians. The main square, called Joy Square, was renamed the Plaza del Armas. Its temples and palaces, built of stone without mortar and covered with beaten gold, were completely razed, and a Spanish cathedral was constructed on the foundations.

In 1654, the grand and austerely beautiful church was ready for use. The paintings and statuary within the cathedral speak eloquently of the mingling of the Old and New World cultures. Alongside Spanish screens and reliquaries are Christian artifacts fashioned by Incan artists: depictions of Christ with unmistakably Indian features and of the Virgin Mary as an Incan or Spanish noblewoman—a poignant reminder of the subjugation of a whole continent to the Cross.

Like Cuzco Cathedral, the church of San Marco in Venice was built not only as a religious edifice but also as a symbol of power. Thanks to a flourishing sea trade, the wealthy independent republic on the Adriatic coast of Italy seemed destined to greatness. In the ninth century, two Venetian merchants stole the remains of Saint Mark from Alexandria in Egypt, and the Apostle was soon firmly established as the patron saint of the city. Three churches were built to house his remains. The last, which still stands today, was begun in 1063. Modeled after the Byzantine Church of the Holy Apostles in Constantinople, it takes the form of a Greek cross crowned by five domes. During the construction of San Marco, Venetian merchants were forbidden to return home without gifts of precious treasures for the church. Gothic pinnacles, tabernacles, and statuary are juxtaposed with Byzantine mosaics and Levantine and Romanesque ornamentation; Renaissance paintings by Titian and Tintoretto exist alongside four bronze horses looted from the Hippodrome in Constantinople, which are possibly the work of the Greek sculptor Lysippus.

In its prominent position next to the Doges' Palace on the Piazza San Marco, the basilica, as it is often called, played a unique role in the life of the Republic of Venice. Today, like the city itself, San Marco is plagued by the problems of sinking foundations and industrial pollution—but fortunately the world is alive to the problems of preserving Venice's priceless monuments and art treasures.

At about the same time as the foundation stone of the present-day basilica was laid, the Babenberg Margrave Leopold I established a community of Benedictine monks at Melk in Lower Austria, one of the earliest residences of the Austrian rulers. In 1089, the Benedictine abbey was founded on a narrow, high ridge overlooking the town and the Danube. Over the centuries the monks amassed a magnificent library of more than 75,000 volumes and 1,800 old manuscripts as well as a collection of sacred relics and other treasures.

The monastery often found itself at the center of Austrian history, although it escaped relatively undamaged during the wars with the Ottoman Turks. Bonaparte stayed there during the Napoleonic Wars, at which time his soldiers took it upon themselves to drink their way through Melk's well-stocked wine cellar.

But the monastery's greatest enemy was always fire. Several times it was badly burned, and in the eighteenth century it was completely rebuilt by Jakob Prandtauer into the splendid Baroque edifice that draws countless tourists to this picturesque town each year. Now only a few monks inhabit the monastery, ministering to the parish and maintaining the school which dates back 1,200 years.

Like other shrines in this volume, Melk stands witness to the spirit of those who built in tribute to their faith. Some might argue, in a more whimsical vein, that we might today be without monumental architecture of any kind if our ancestors had not nurtured a religious conscience. This line of reasoning recalls a succinct argument advanced by Voltaire: "If God did not exist, it would have been necessary to invent Him" (Epistle 96).

Cathedral of San Marco

Venice

The Piazza San Marco (preceding page) has been the center of Venetian life since the ninth century when a small church was built there to house the relics of Saint Mark the Evangelist, which were stolen from Alexandria in Egypt by two enterprising local merchants. The present cathedral of San Marco stands adjacent to the Doges' Palace, completed in the fifteenth century. In this magnificent Gothic palace, the elected head of the Venetian state lived as a virtual prisoner of the populace.

The cathedral was maintained by the procurators of San Marco. Above left, the Procuratie, the fifteenth- and sixteenth-century headquarters of these magistrates, which lines three sides of the piazza. Seen from across the piazza, the cathedral is dominated by the 324-foot Campanile (below left). The original bell tower, which was begun in the tenth century and was constructed over a period of 500 years, collapsed in 1902. Miraculously, no one was injured, and the façade of the basilica—as the cathedral is called, though technically it is not basilic in form—escaped damage. The Venetians immediately reconstructed the Campanile exactly as it had been in a spirit of thanksgiving.

The Oriental flavor of Venetian architecture, evident even in the fifteenth-century galleries of the Doges' Palace (center right), reflects a heritage of the city's early alliance and long trading relationship with Byzantium. Bottom right, the library by the prominent architect-sculptor Jacopo Sansovino, seen through the arcade of the Doges' Palace. The cathedral itself (top right) was modeled after the Church of the Holy Apostles in Constantinople.

Five lantern-capped domes mark the four equal arms and central intersection of the Greek-cross plan of San Marco. Though San Marco is recognized as being the finest Byzantine church still in use, it is a Roman Catholic shrine. Under the rule of the doges, however, papal authority never carried much weight in Venice. The senate of the Republic of St. Mark exercised strict control over the clergy, and until early in the sixteenth century, erring priests were publicly punished by imprisonment in an iron cage suspended from one side of the Campanile.

Celebrated in local legend as "the two Moors," a pair of mallet-wielding bronze statues strikes the hour atop a fifteenth-century clock tower of the piazza. Medieval and Renaissance Venice was known throughout Europe for its substantial Middle Eastern and North African population, a reputation which inspired Shakespeare's Othello. *These statues of the Moors, however, came by their name as a result of the coating of soot and corrosion that has darkened them over the centuries; the artist intended the figures to represent "men of the greenwood."*

Venetian notables customarily gathered on the balcony encircling the upper part of the façade of San Marco (above and above right) for a better view of the jousting tournaments, bullfights, and triumphal processions that were staged in the piazza below. At this level, the fantastic decorative detail is clearly evident, including Gothic sculpture and pinnacles as well as lunette mosaics executed between the thirteenth and nineteenth centuries. All merge compatibly with the essentially Byzantine flavor of the façade.

The Victorian writer and cultural critic John Ruskin delighted in the Oriental splendor of the western façade of San Marco, a far cry from the "grim" cathedrals of England. Ruskin's ideas profoundly influenced the taste of his fellow Victorians. He especially commended the playful corner arches (left), thoroughly approving of the fact that they have no function except to consummate the proportions of the façade.

Below, a detail of the intricate bronze gateway of the Loggetta, which stands at the base of the Campanile facing the cathedral. Built from 1537 to 1549 as a meeting place for the nobility, it was later rebuilt by Jacopo Sansovino. The bronze work of the gates is by the sculptor Antonio Gay and dates from the eighteenth century.

Above left, Saint George, one of four warrior-saints atop the pinnacles of the western façade. The statue epitomizes the martial aspect of the façade, whose central portal bears a striking resemblance to a triumphal arch. Part of the booty brought home by the navy of medieval Venice are the four tetrarchs, sculpted around A.D. *305 from Egyptian porphyry. The group (one pair shown center left and right) represents the four co-rulers of the Roman Empire who embrace each other to confirm their hopes—never realized—for eventual unity. Above and below, the bronze horses above the main arch, looted from the Hippodrome in Constantinople during the Fourth Crusade.*

During the construction of San Marco, the doge issued an edict forbidding any Venetian merchant to return home without bringing some treasure to ornament the new church. The resulting influx of gifts included variegated building stones of jasper, red porphyry, and white-flecked green serpentine marble, sculpted capitals and bases in every conceivable mode, and decorative window screens from the Levant (above right and right).

Left, a section of Sansovino's Loggetta, which exhibits a remarkably rich but precise Classical style that developed in Venice during the Renaissance years.

San Marco is the most richly decorated church in Christendom. The vault mosaics (above left, above, and right) alone took seven centuries to complete and reflect a sweep of historical styles from high Byzantine to late Renaissance. Below left, the double pulpit whose lower tier is for Epistle readings and the upper for the Gospel. While the pulpit recalls Moslem constructions inside mosques of Asia Minor, the Gothic crucifix and freestanding statues mounted on the chancel screen are entirely Western.

VA FIT VINVM EX GRATIA FEMINAE MIRVM
SANCTVS PETRVS
FLENT TVMVLANTES
RANT EXIT CITATIS

The sixteenth-century Apocalypse arch (above) in the foreground contrasts with the more serene and stylized Pentecost cupola in the background and the magnificent Creation cupola (right). The latter, dating from ca. 1200, was probably inspired by a fourth-century illuminated manuscript. Below, the mid-fourteenth-century mosaics of the baptistery annex.

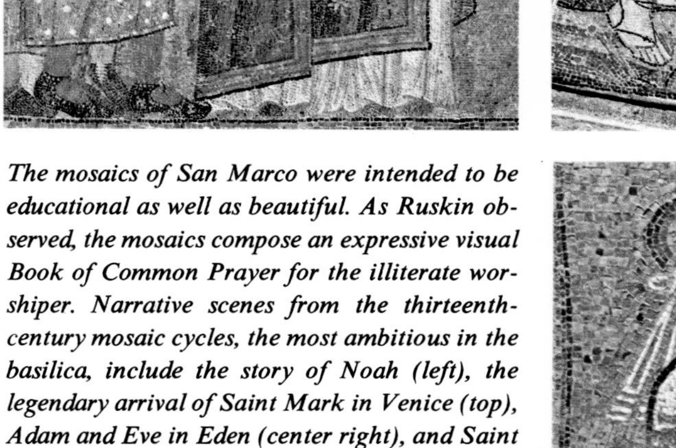

The mosaics of San Marco were intended to be educational as well as beautiful. As Ruskin observed, the mosaics compose an expressive visual Book of Common Prayer for the illiterate worshiper. Narrative scenes from the thirteenth-century mosaic cycles, the most ambitious in the basilica, include the story of Noah (left), the legendary arrival of Saint Mark in Venice (top), Adam and Eve in Eden (center right), and Saint Hilarion (bottom right).

Studded with a fortune in precious stones, the fabulous Pala d'Oro (above right) occupies the place of honor on the front of the basilica's high altar. This gold screen, mostly the work of eleventh- and twelfth-century artists, incorporates over 100 enameled miniatures as well as 1,300 pearls, 300 sapphires, 300 emeralds, and 400 garnets. All of the original gems were cabochons (highly polished, unfaceted gems). The faceted emerald seen at the top of the panel (left) replaced a stone taken by the soldiers of Napoleon when they occupied Venice in 1797. Right, detail of the Pala d'Oro, showing the Entry into Jerusalem, the Resurrection, and the Crucifixion.

Following page, the Lion of St. Mark the Evangelist, the symbol of the Venetian Republic. This winged beast, brought to Venice from the East, surveys the harbor from his red granite column near the Doges' Palace.

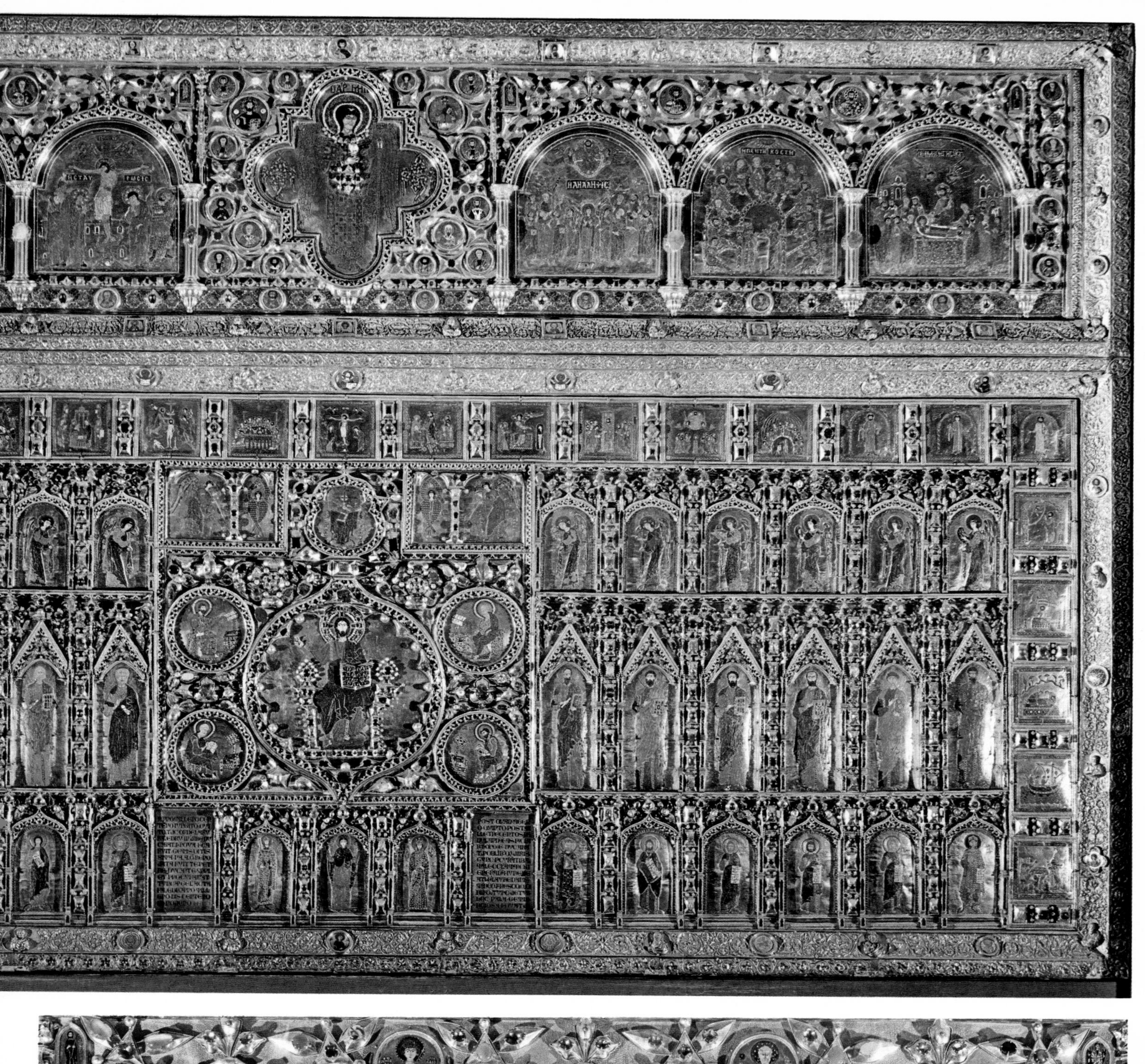

ΗΒΑΙΟΦΟΡΟС
ΗΑΝΑСΤΑСΙС
ΙС ХС
ΗСΤΑΥ ΡΩСΙС

Cathedral of San Marco Venice

Venice is a European city with an Oriental sense of pageantry. This independent republic, built on a lagoon off the coast of Italy, has garnered more titles than an Eastern potentate, among them the Republic of St. Mark, La Serenissima, Queen of the Adriatic, and the Bride of the Sea. Nor was this last a mere figure of speech. Every year on Ascension Day, in a procession attended by thousands of visitors from all over Europe, the city formally reconsecrated its marriage vows in an elaborate ritual that culminated in the ceremony of the "marriage to the sea." Beginning with a prayer of dedication inside the cathedral, the doge of Venice and his fellow celebrants would progress down to the water's edge where, at the appointed moment, the doge would fling a gold ring into the lagoon in observance of the harmonious partnership between the city and the sea.

Venice was also conscientious about honoring its patron, Saint Mark the Evangelist. Venetian merchants and sailors carried the banner bearing the Lion of St. Mark into ports all over the known world, and in the city itself the evangelist's emblem was—and is still—ubiquitous. Artists of every degree of talent have commemorated the lion emblem in stone, bronze, mosaic, and paint.

San Marco and Venice have been closely associated for so long that many people are surprised to learn that the city's original patron was not Saint Mark at all but the Greek Saint Theodore. On the other hand, no one familiar with the Venetian republic's history of political intrigue and aggressive commercial tactics is shocked to learn how the switch came about. Dissatisfied with their original protector, the Venetians simply set out to steal the evangelist—body and soul as it were—from Alexandria in Egypt. The move was especially daring considering that Alexandria was a Moslem port, prohibited to Christian mariners.

The theft occurred in 828 when two merchants, Rustico Torcello and Buono da Malamocco, managed to bribe the keeper of the evangelist's tomb. Alerted by an overpoweringly sweet odor that filled the city as soon as the tomb was opened, the Moslem population of Alexandria searched the city for the missing relics, even as the merchants were stashing the bones in a basket of pickled pork and making their escape. Thus disguised, Saint Mark was carried to Venice, where he was deposited in the Doges' Palace until the first church of San Marco was finished several years later. Four hundred years after the saint's abduction, when the Venetians were embellishing the present

The lagoon teems with activity in this 1492 woodcut by a monk, Filippo da Bergamo. In the background are the domes of San Marco rising above the Doges' Palace.

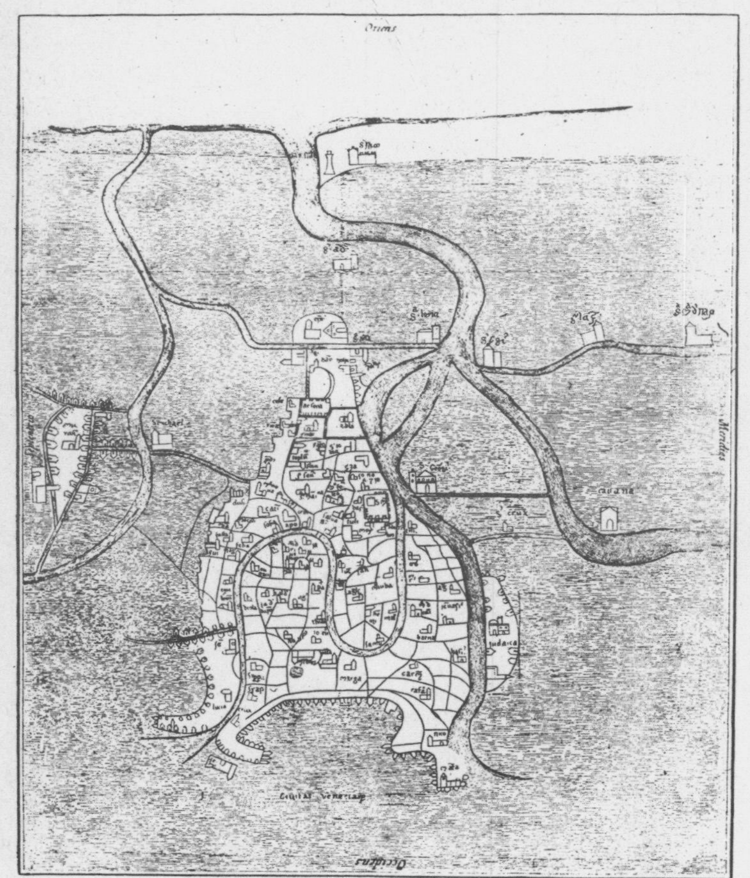

Above, a fifteenth-century miniature from the Book of Marco Polo *in the Bodleain Library, Oxford. This print is probably the oldest representation of the Piazza San Marco. The unknown miniaturist probably never even saw the piazza which he depicted so vividly; he may have heard tales of a marvelous church on a festive golden square peopled with brightly dressed nobles.*

Above, a seventh-century plan of Venice. Below, an eighteenth-century sketch showing the new basilica beside the old fortified Doges' Palace, as it might have looked in the mid-twelfth century.

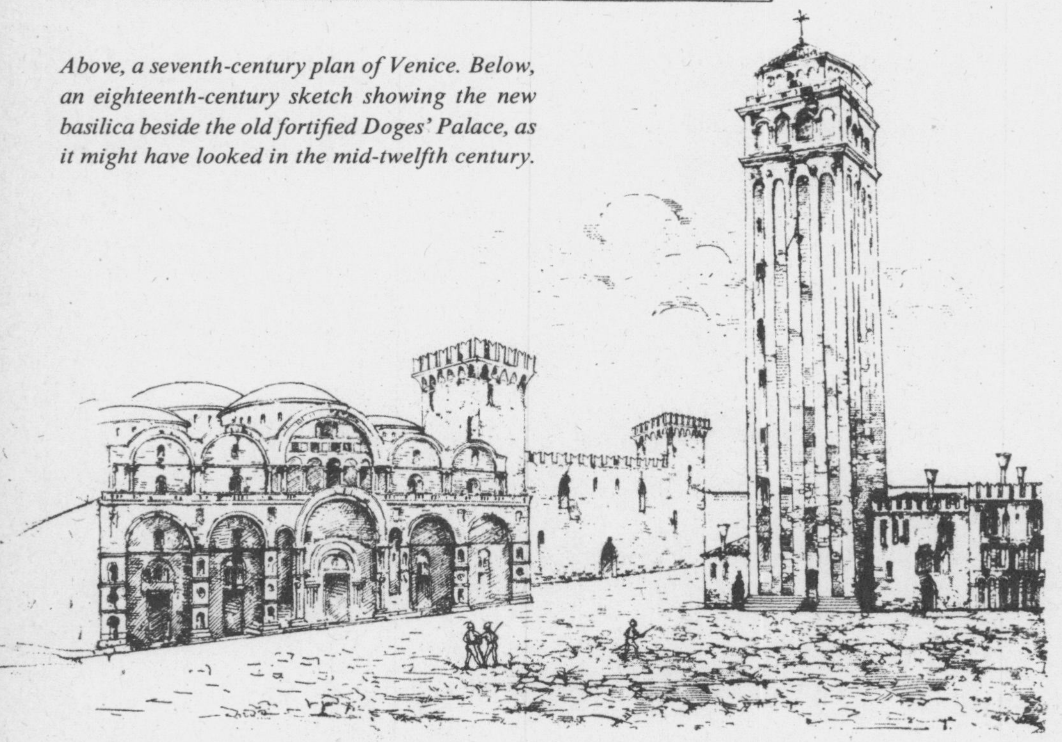

church, a legend of predestination arose justifying the theft. According to the story, Saint Mark had once been shipwrecked off the Venetian coast when an angel appeared to him saying, "Peace be unto you, Mark, my Evangelist. Know that here thy body shall rest." This legend was so similar to other prevalent stories about shipwrecked holy men that to question it would have meant casting doubt on the authenticity of half the patron saints of the Mediterranean. In any case, Venice's adoption of Saint Mark carried a clear political message: The republic now had a symbol worthy of a place beside the coat of arms of any royal family in Europe.

Although Saint Mark won quick acceptance as the protector of the republic, two centuries passed before he was honored by a suitably important church. The original San Marco, consecrated in 832, had been little more than a private chapel of the doge, and as a result of this identification with the head of state, it was burned to the ground in 976 during a popular rebellion against Doge Pietro Candiano IV. Little is known of the second San Marco, built on the same site by Doge Pietro Orseolo I.

But by the time construction began on the third and final church of San Marco in 1063, Venice and the evangelist were ready for a more substantial monument. A few years before, the Holy Roman and Byzantine empires had finally recognized the autonomy of the republic. The city, whose fleet included more than sixty large vessels, was then able to expand its military and commercial horizons. Now, as work on the third San Marco got under way, the ruling doge, Domenico Selvo, arranged to tap the new wealth flowing into

Venice by issuing an edict that forbade any Venetian merchant to return from the East without including in his cargo some precious stones, gold, or other treasures for the church.

Doge Selvo, a great admirer of Byzantine art, may have been responsible for the decision to pattern this new San Marco after the Church of the Holy Apostles in Constantinople, which shelters the tombs of the Apostles Luke, Andrew, and Timothy. In any case, the choice was a natural one, for ties between Venice and Byzantium had always been close. Thus, the Roman Catholic San Marco acquired the characteristic form of an Eastern rite church: four arms of equal length joined in the center of the resultant Greek cross, with a dome surmounting each arm and a fifth dome atop the intersection of the arms.

As is true for many Western cathedrals, the architect responsible for setting down the final design of San Marco is unknown. Tradition says that he is represented in the third arch of the western façade, where there is a figure of a cripple holding his index finger to his lips in a gesture of silence. The architect, reputedly crippled by a fall from the dome scaffolding, is supposed to have made a bet with the doge who promised to pay him a fortune if everyone agreed that the finished domes were flawless. The architect would have won, so the story goes, except that one day the doge happened to overhear him criticizing his own work, and the architect lost his fortune.

The architect's own ill-timed disparagement aside, San Marco is a universally acclaimed architectural masterpiece. Often called simply a basilica, the church is widely accepted as the finest Byzantine-style church in Western Europe and one of the finest ever built anywhere. San Marco cannot really be considered the work of a single architect. A number of master builders were involved in the original project, and long after the church was consecrated in 1094, Gothic pinnacles, turrets, statuary, and other decorative touches were added to the main façade. Similarly, the mosaic decorations of the interior were not completed until the sixteenth century, hundreds of years after the original Byzantine mosaicists were dead and buried. In fact, embellishing and maintaining San Marco came to be such an all-consuming enterprise that it was necessary to house church-related activities in the building on the north side of the piazza.

Despite the overlays of Levantine, Romanesque, Gothic, and even Renaissance decorations, the essentially Byzantine character of the basilica was never obscured. The difference in historical styles is less dramatic than the contrast between the exterior and interior of the church. The journalist James Morris once commented that San Marco was "descended from Byzantium, by faith, out of nationalism," and the most obvious result of this mixed ancestry is that the western façade of the church resembles a patriotic monument rather than a religious shrine. Warrior saints and representations of Hercules embellish the façade, and on the central portal, a bronze quartet of ancient Greek horses looks suspiciously like a triumphal arch. The horses were probably cast in Corinth around 2,200 years ago by the Greek sculptor Lysippus. The martial aspect of these magnificent horses attracted the attention of several famous rulers, all of whom had them transported to their own monuments. The practice was initiated by the Roman Emperor Nero, who had them placed on his triumphal arch in A.D. 68. Constantine later had them

Above, Doge Francisco Donato, portrayed by Titian. Right, an eighteenth-century print showing the south façade of San Marco as it appears from the interior courtyard of the Doges' Palace.

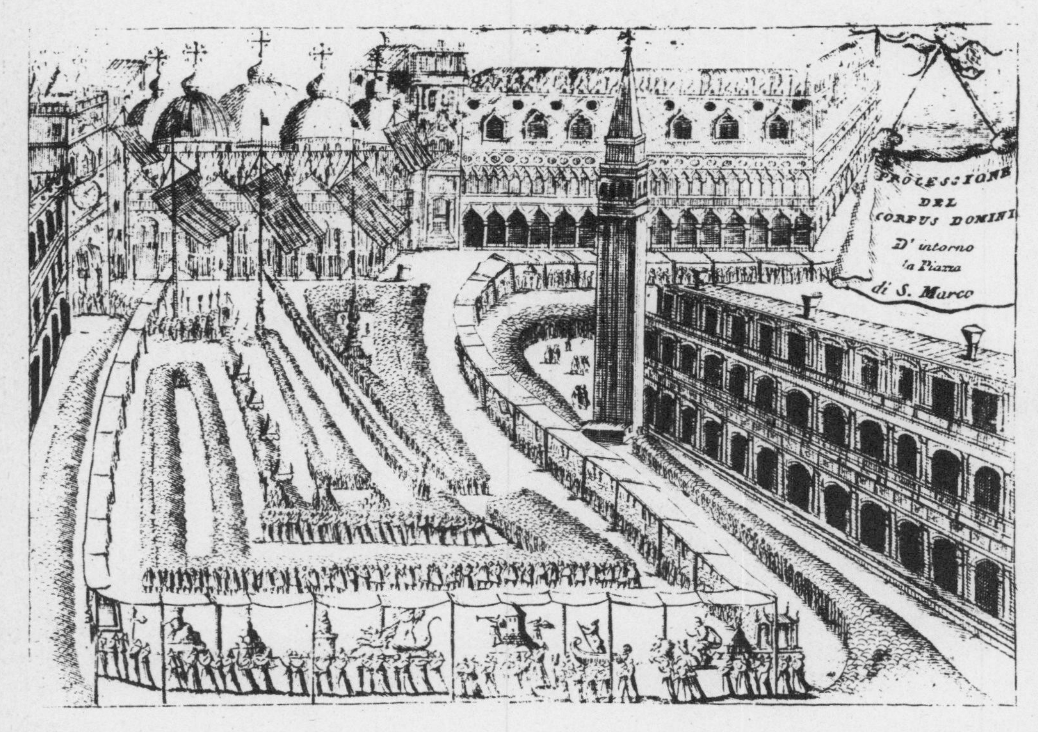

The banners of Venice's three medieval colonies fly before the basilica as an enormous Corpus Christi Day procession snakes through the piazza (above). Other festivities included Carnival (below right) and performances by traveling theater groups (bottom right). Jacopo Sansovino (below left) was the last great procurator of San Marco and was responsible for the Loggetta of the Campanile. Bottom left, Titian's portrait of Doge Venier.

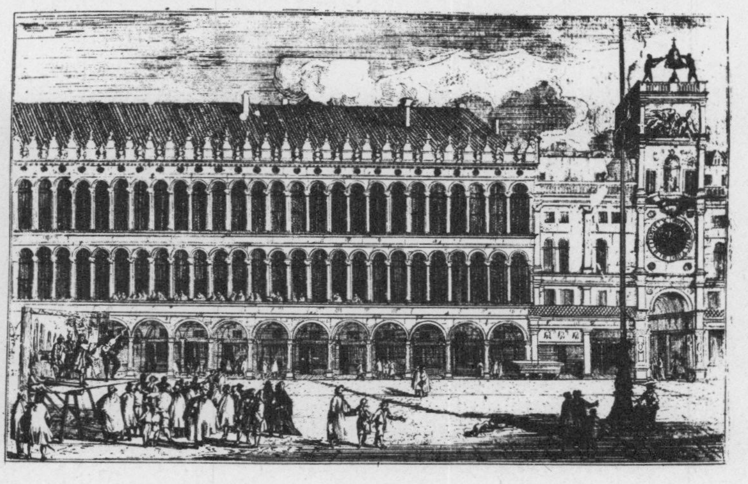

moved to Constantinople, where they embellished the Hippodrome. The bronze quartet remained there for almost 900 years, until Doge Enrico Dandolo seized the horses as war booty during the Fourth Crusade (1203). At his express command, the horses were carried to Venice in honor of its patron saint.

The military overtones of the façade of San Marco express the church's unique role in the life of the Venetian republic. In the absence of a royal palace, the basilica served as the backdrop for civic pageants and ceremonies staged in the piazza. Here, Venetian sea captains assumed their commands before undertaking ambitious missions at sea, and here they celebrated their naval victories. Petrarch, writing in the fourteenth century, told of sitting next to the reigning doge on the basilica's elevated balcony to watch a jousting tournament conducted in the piazza below. Bullfights, carnivals, and even public executions have all been staged in the piazza at one time or another, but the most important and unusual ceremony ever held here took place in 1177, not long after the piazza had been enlarged to its present size. In that year, Doge Sebastiano Ziani arranged a humiliating public reconciliation between the Emperor Frederick Barbarossa, whom he had just defeated in a great naval battle, and the emperor's erstwhile enemy Pope Alexander III. It is said that when Frederick knelt as ordered to kiss the pope's foot, he was heard to mutter under his breath, "Not to thee, but to Saint Peter," whereupon Alexander placed his foot on the emperor's neck and forced him to pay homage with the words "for me *and* Saint Peter." Of course, the real victor of the day was Venice, which had proved its ability to play a pivotal role in Mediterranean power politics.

If the exterior of the basilica exalts the destiny of the Republic of St. Mark, the interior suggests the mystery of faith. The darkest part of the nave lies just inside the main portal. As the worshiper enters, his gaze is led inevitably toward the eastern sanctuary where thin, brilliant shafts of light stream down from the cupola win-

dows. The varying quality of the light, which illuminates different art works according to the time of day, prevents the rich, eclectic ornamentation from degenerating into materialistic spectacle.

Even a skeptic would have to admit that the nave is the perfect setting for a miracle. As it happened, medieval Venice had more than its share of skeptics, and when a miracle occurred here in the year 1094, it was aimed directly at them—although whether it was the work of God or some other interested party is open to question. During the years when San Marco was under construction, there was much speculation about the relics of Saint Mark the Evangelist, which had been missing since the first church was destroyed by fire in 976. To stem rumors of their possible loss, which might lead to a decrease in revenue, a special service was held to ask God's guidance in finding Saint Mark's earthly remains. Almost as soon as the service began, a powerful perfume filled the basilica and two stones in the base of one of the chapel altars creaked open to reveal an apparition. Later, some members of the congregation swore that they had seen Saint Mark himself step from the opening and raise his hand in blessing. Others claimed that nothing had emerged but a skeleton displayed in a coffin. In any event, everyone agreed that the evangelist was now officially in residence, and the spot where he manifested himself was marked with a marble tablet which remains in place to this day.

Besides a ceremonial square, the Piazza San Marco (above) has also been a place for Venetians to rendezvous and for merchants to display their wares.

Venice's annual marriage to the sea is celebrated in The Departure of the Bucintoro *by Guardi (below). Here, the doge crosses the lagoon in a ceremonial boat, the* bucintoro, *to fling a gold wedding ring into the Adriatic.*

The mosaics of San Marco, which cover virtually every square inch of the vault ceilings and walls, have earned the cathedral its appellation of the Chiesa d'Oro, or Golden Church. The mosaics took over six centuries to complete and are perhaps the greatest single display of that art form anywhere in the world. The earlier cycles, such as the vault mosaics that depict scenes from the Creation and Genesis, were probably inspired by early illuminated manuscripts and represent a conscious adherence to Byzantine aesthetics. It was these cycles which attracted the admiration of the Victorian critic John Ruskin, who argued that their highly stylized iconography was superior to Renaissance realism because it expressed a concern with the innate nature of the objects portrayed rather than with mere earthly forms. After the thirteenth century, when the art of mosaic working began to die out in Constantinople, it continued to flourish in Venice. Influenced by the Gothic, Venetian masters gradually introduced more expressive, humanistic figures. By the time the basilica's mosaics were completed, the Renaissance was at its height, and the last generation of artists to contribute designs included Titian, Tintoretto, Veronese, and Bassano.

Even as these great sixteenth-century painters were leaving their stamp on San Marco under the direction of its last notable procurator, Jacopo Sansovino, Venice itself began to exhibit the first signs of its long decline. The discovery of America and of new trade routes to the East eclipsed Venice's commanding position as the commercial gateway to the Orient. One by one, Venice also lost its three medieval colonies—Cyprus, Crete, and the Peloponnese—requiring that the banners of the provinces, once prominently displayed in the three red flagpoles in front of San Marco, be replaced by ceremonial flags. Outwardly, Venice was more beautiful than ever, but as its power drained away, the draconian machinery of the republic, to which the Venetians had long ago sacrificed so many personal liberties for civic independence, began to degenerate into an instrument of dark intrigues.

During this century of petty conspiracies, Venice developed a taste for frivolity. Everyone, from peasant to doge, adopted the custom of going about the city masked, and the most fashionable Venetian ladies even wore their disguises while attending services at San Marco. (Some historians have suggested that the widespread use of

Standing beneath the Lion of St. Mark, Napoleon Bonaparte orders the dissolution of the hundred-year-old Venetian republic (below).

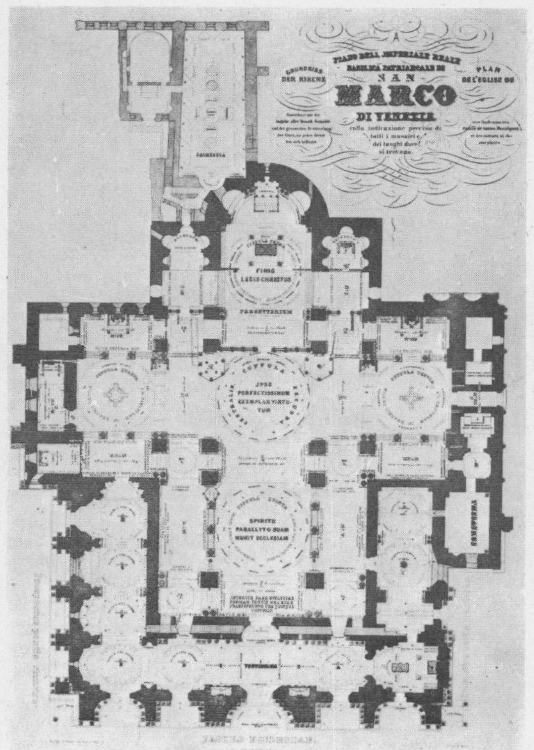

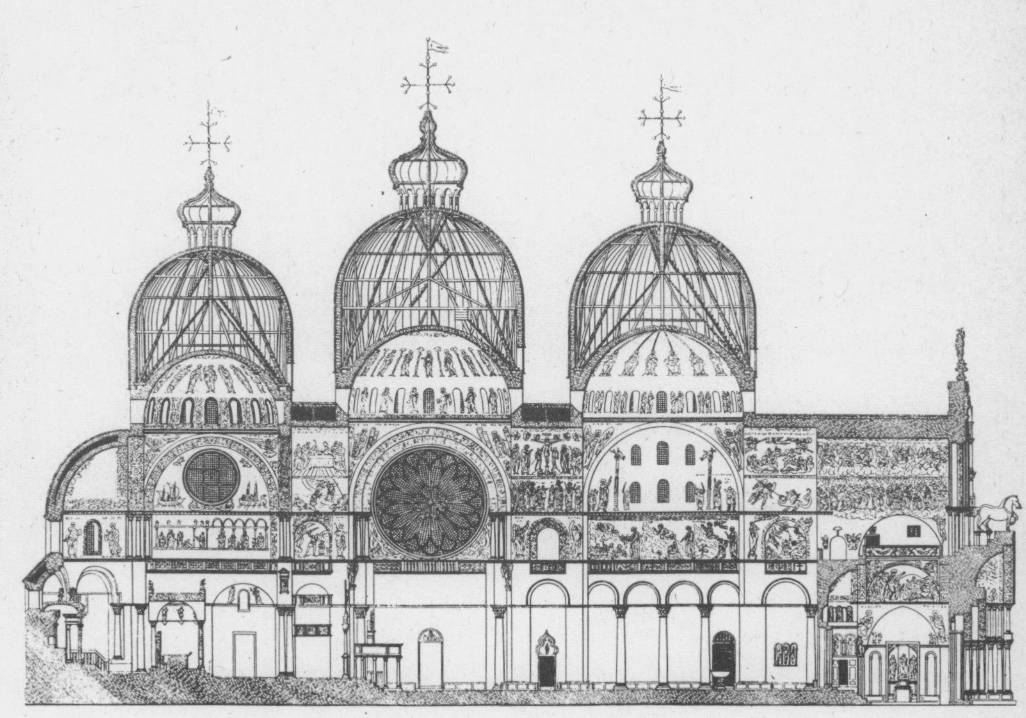

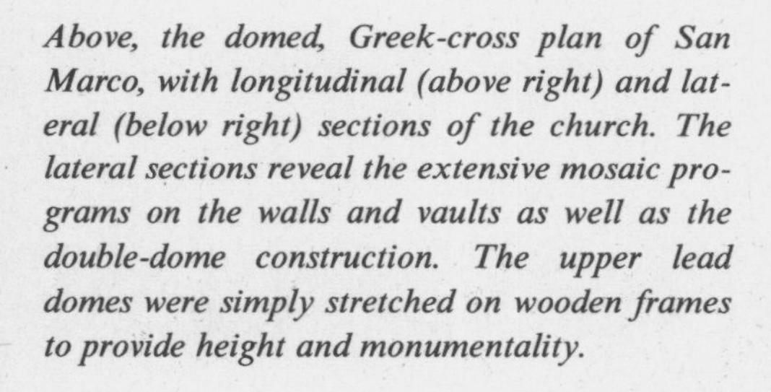

Above, the domed, Greek-cross plan of San Marco, with longitudinal (above right) and lateral (below right) sections of the church. The lateral sections reveal the extensive mosaic programs on the walls and vaults as well as the double-dome construction. The upper lead domes were simply stretched on wooden frames to provide height and monumentality.

lead-based make-up and wig powder contributed to skin disorders which encouraged the use of masks.)

By the eighteenth century, Venice was renowned as the most decadent city in Europe. The home of Marco Polo, of Titian and Veronese, and of the world's longest established republic was now best known as the pagan playground of Casanova. Still wealthy–mainly because of landholdings–but only going through the motions of power politics, the city attracted the attention of Napoleon Bonaparte, who vowed to make the Venetians pay for his Italian campaigns. Recalling the old legend that Venice had been founded by people from the mainland fleeing across the lagoons to escape the hordes of Attila the Hun, Napoleon declared, "I will be an Attila to the State of Venice." And he was. French troops entered the city in the summer of 1797, stripping jewels from the gold altar screen of the basilica and carting off its four bronze horses for display in Paris.

After Waterloo, the magnificent ancient quartet was returned to its place of honor over the basilica's doorway. In the twentieth century, however, these survivors have become witnesses to Venice's latest struggle–against the forces of nature and the effects of industrialization. The century began with an ill omen. On July 14, 1902, the Campanile, Venice's tallest and most vulnerable landmark, collapsed in a heap of rubble. The bell tower's demise shocked the Venetians, who had christened the commanding tower "the Landlord." Fortunately, the 324-foot tower fell in such a way that the nearby western façade of San Marco was spared. (The weathervane landed just a few feet away from the main door of the basilica.) An exact copy of the Campanile was completed by 1912, in time for the thousandth anniversary celebration of the founding of the original tower.

This incident was just a harbinger of a

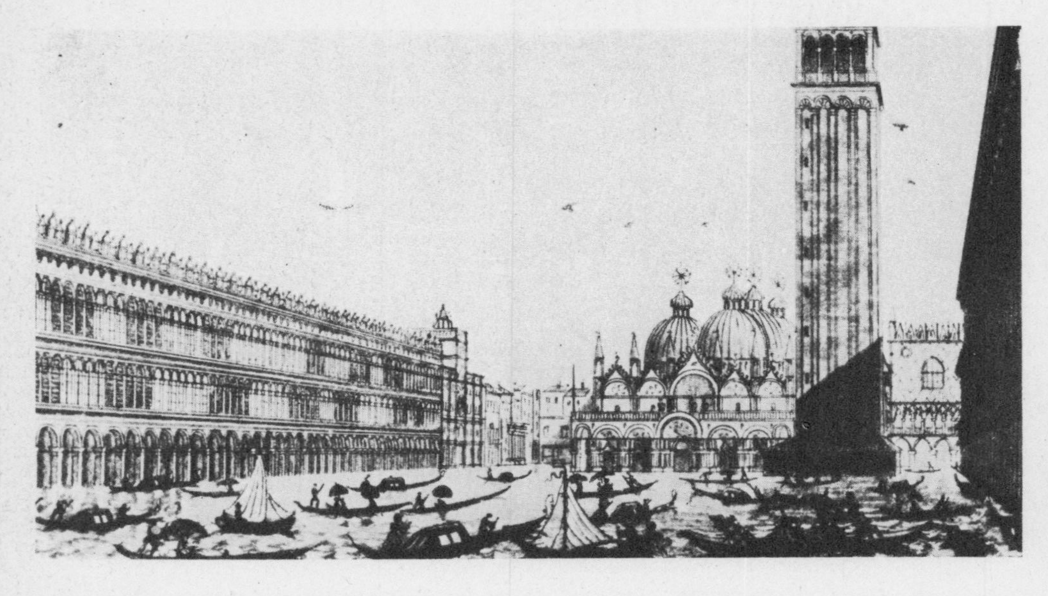

Flooding has long been a problem for Venice. This early nineteenth-century print shows boats plying their way through the heart of the Piazza San Marco.

Below, a panoramic view of Venice in the early eighteenth century by Vincenzo Coronelli, who was the official cosmographer of the republic.

more ominous threat. Engineers soon began to warn that all of Venice was slowly sinking into its mud foundations, and the city was confronted with the urgent task of preserving its monuments. It now appears that this battle will be won, partly due to a natural process that is maintaining the waters at a manageable level. But Venice faces yet another challenge–industrial pollution from nearby factories is eroding the statues and buildings of the old city at an alarming rate.

Today, the sea is no longer Venice's husband, but her enemy. On the other hand, the city's plight has made her the focus of an international rescue operation and a laboratory for the development of new restoration techniques that may eventually help to save priceless monuments in many countries of the industrialized world. And at the heart of this beleaguered city, the basilica attracts more attention than it has for centuries. It is difficult to imagine that devotees of Renaissance aesthetics once condemned San Marco as "barbaric" and that they even proposed tearing it down. As late as 1848, John Ruskin complained that, "You may walk from sunrise to sunset, to and fro, before the Gateway of St. Mark's, and you will not see an eye lifted to it, nor a countenance brightened by it." Although the church still has its critics–one of whom recently compared it to "a Mongolian pleasure palace"–such purists are now in the distinct minority.

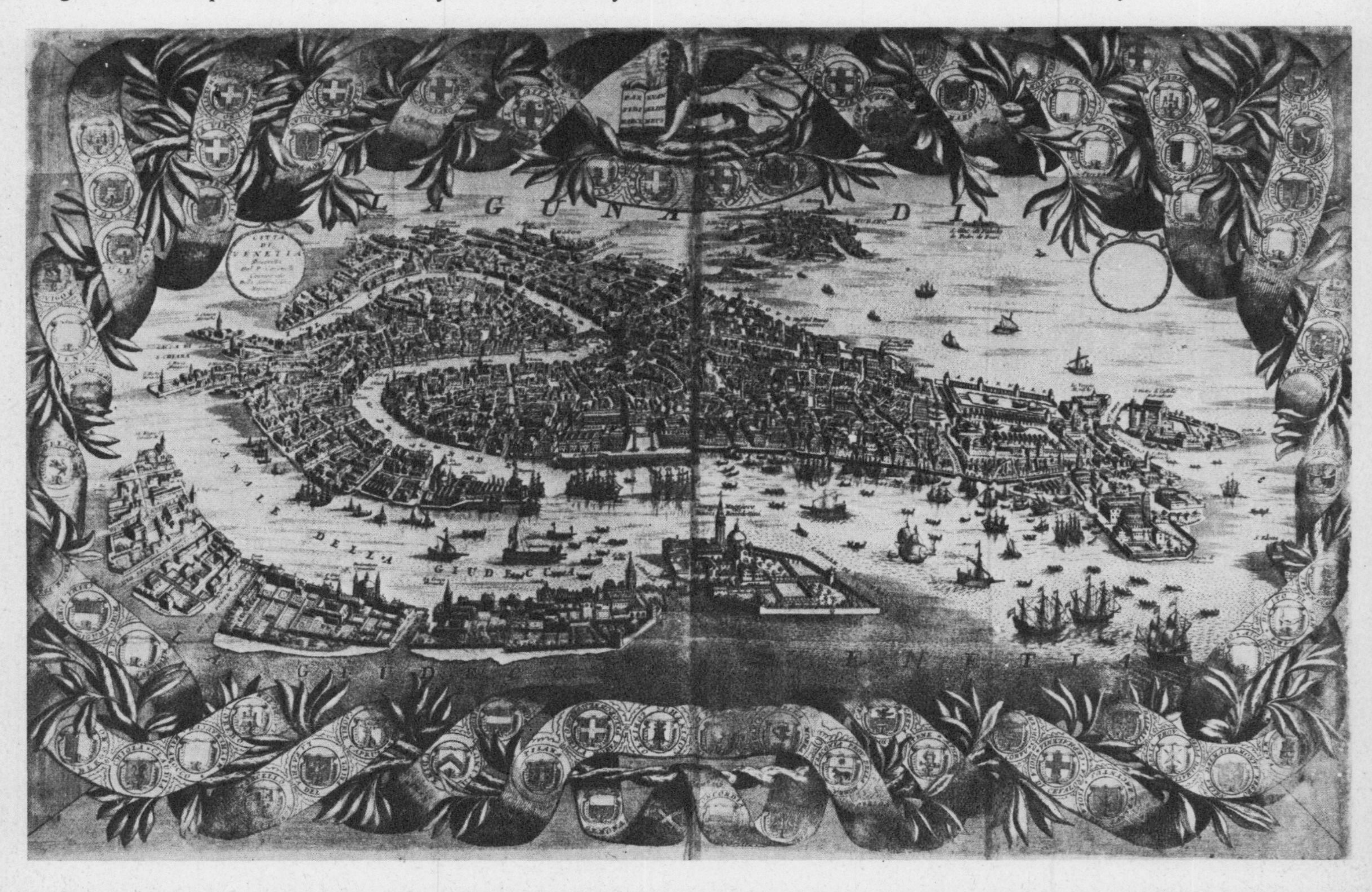

Notre Dame

Paris

Notre Dame de Paris (preceding page), the dowager queen of French cathedrals, was inspired by the learned religious philosopher Abbot Suger, who believed that religious architecture should use "Divine Light" almost as if it were a construction material. Dramatic flying buttresses, pointed arches, and large expanses of stained glass came to be the hallmarks of the new style. This well-known view of the cathedral from the left bank of the Seine reveals the pointed flèche (spire), the southern rose window, and the baptistery annex to the left of the chapel, all reconstructed in the nineteenth century by the French theorist Eugène Viollet-le-Duc.

Notre Dame's western façade (left) is a classic statement of Gothic concepts of harmony and geometric order. The parvis, or forecourt of the cathedral, was cleared during the last century by the removal of several medieval buildings. The façade's twin towers (top right) are linked by the Grand Gallery, an elegant stone arcade.

The Holy Virgin, holding the Christ child and flanked by a pair of angels (above), stands in the place of honor before the great western rose window. Below her, in the Gallery of Kings (center right), are twenty-eight rulers of Israel and Judea. The original statues were decapitated during the French Revolution by an anti-Royalist mob.

Portal sculpture provided a veritable encyclopedia of Christian personages and dogma. The Royal Portal (bottom right) portrays the Last Judgment, the Wise and Foolish Virgins, the twelve Apostles, Christ teaching, and the entire register of the heavenly court.

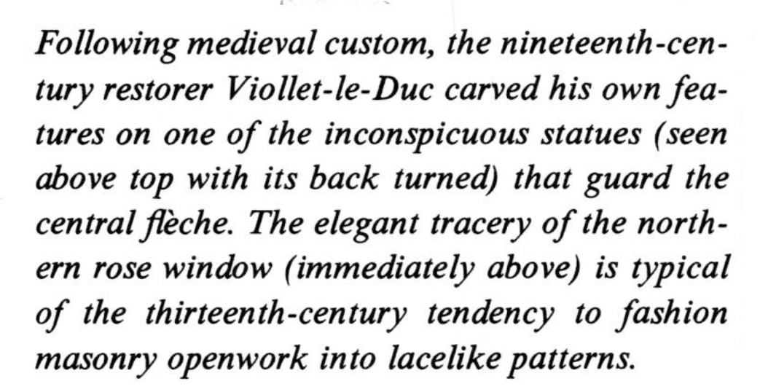

Following medieval custom, the nineteenth-century restorer Viollet-le-Duc carved his own features on one of the inconspicuous statues (seen above top with its back turned) that guard the central flèche. The elegant tracery of the northern rose window (immediately above) is typical of the thirteenth-century tendency to fashion masonry openwork into lacelike patterns.

The flying buttress (above right and right) first appeared as an architectural structure at Notre Dame. These arched supports, rising above the main buttresses, were used to receive the thrust of high Gothic vaults and channel it down to the ground.

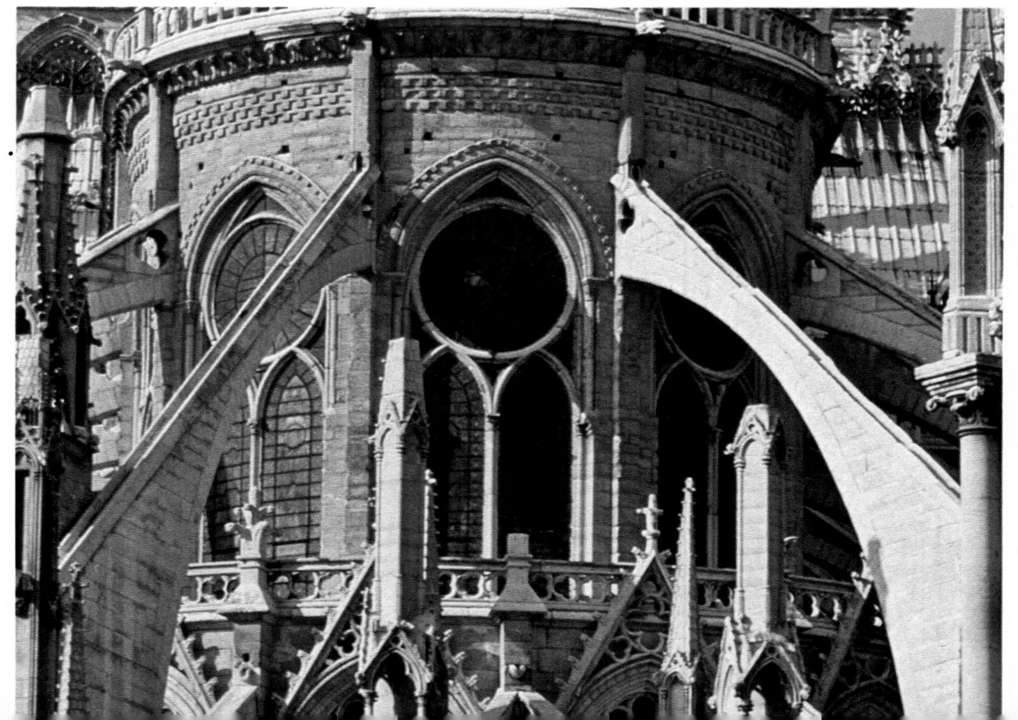

Medieval sculptors gave free reign to their imaginations in creating grotesque gargoyles. Intended as run-off spouts for rainwater, these figures were not subject to the rigid iconographic restrictions that governed the forms of the façade's religious statuary. A medieval legend says that Notre Dame's gargoyles were the work of a deformed sculptor who nursed a hopeless passion for the wife of one of the cathedral's glaziers. One day the woman's husband tried to throw his pitiful rival into the Seine, but the Virgin herself intervened, and the sculptor returned to the lonely work of fashioning monsters that mirrored his own physical deformities. Many of the Notre Dame gargoyles shown here are modern copies based on drawings of the originals.

The interior of the Gothic cathedral (facing page) represents the Heavenly Jerusalem, illuminated by divine revelation. The use of stained glass enacted this metaphor by transforming ordinary sunlight into a miraculous rainbow of color. The northern rose window (above left) was reconstructed by Viollet-le-Duc, who employed modern chemical analysis to reconstruct the lost formulas of medieval glaziers. The southern rose window (above right) is the original thirteenth-century masterpiece by Jean de Chelles. Below, interior details of Notre Dame (left to right): sexpartite vaults, a pseudo-Corinthian capital from the tribune, and windows depicting the life of Christ from one of the side aisle chapels.

In a striking contrast to the weighty and dignified western façade, a view of Notre Dame from the east (following page) dramatically reveals the use of flying buttresses to encircle and support the high choir.

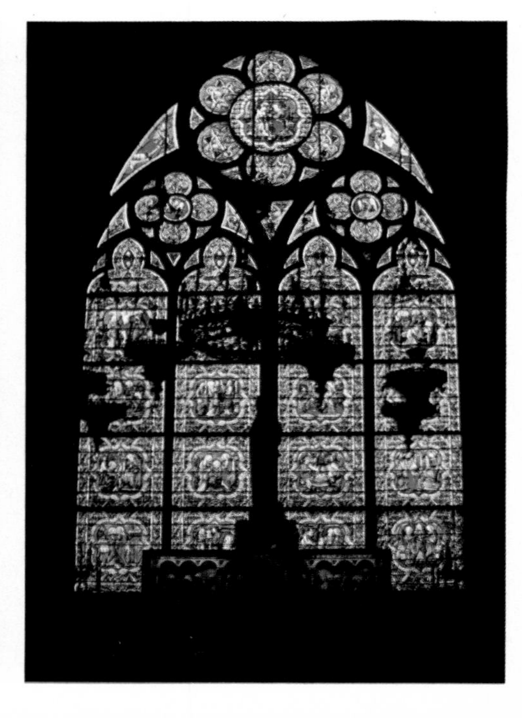

Notre Dame Paris

"The last illusion remaining to me was a cathedral, and now they have destroyed it." This was François René de Châteaubriand's melancholy reaction to Victor Hugo's novel *The Hunchback of Notre Dame* (1831). Although Hugo's use of the historic cathedral as a background for his tale of a deformed bell ringer depressed his literary mentor Châteaubriand, the reading public reacted quite differently. Set in the fifteenth century during the reign of Louis XI, when Notre Dame was still the spiritual focus of Parisian life, the novel pointedly called attention to its state of disrepair in the nineteenth century. Hugo's pleas in behalf of the medieval church opened the public's eyes to the beauties of tradition and won support for an energetic restoration campaign.

Although few major architectural styles can be traced to a specific point of origin, the Île de France can justly claim to be the birthplace of the Gothic cathedral. The Gothic era was inaugurated not in Paris itself but several miles northwest of the city proper, at the royal abbey church of St. Denis. In the early twelfth century, St. Denis became the seat of the remarkable Abbot Suger, the most trusted political adviser of Louis VI.

One of Suger's greatest loves was architecture, and in 1125, he revealed his plans to reconstruct his decaying Carolingian church with a new narthex and a new, much larger choir. Suger proclaimed that churches should be so proportioned as to represent the Creation in miniature. Further, the abbot argued that "Divine Light" was evidence of God's presence. This "miraculous" sunlight was to be used, according to Suger, as if it were an actual building material.

Suger's vision was made possible by a number of technical developments, especially the introduction of the pointed arch, which was more flexible and stronger with less outward thrust than the rounded Romanesque arch. Part of the credit for this innovation must go to the Crusaders, who probably brought the idea for the pointed arch back with them from the East. Credit must also go to the anonymous master masons who supplied the technical expertise to realize Suger's theories in concrete form at St. Denis.

Whatever its origins, the new style Suger had created for his abbey church soon found its fullest expression in the urban cathedral. The twelfth century was a prosperous time, and so many cities and towns built new cathedrals that, as one chronicler wrote, "It was almost as if the world had shaken off its old clothes and covered itself with a white vestment of churches."

The laying of the cornerstone of Suger's church in 1144 was a sumptuous occasion, made even more memorable by Louis VII's impulsive decision to throw one of his gold rings into the wet mortar. Etiquette required the rest of the court to follow his example, and even Louis's less pious queen, Eleanor of Aquitaine, sacrificed a piece of jewelry to consecrate the project. Among the less conspicuous witnesses to this royal drama was the Archdeacon Maurice de Sully who, like Suger, was destined to rise far above his peasant origins to high ecclesiastical office. In his private life, Sully was the most unassuming of men, well known for his ascetic habits and his devotion to the poor. Nevertheless, Suger's project made a strong impression on him, and when Sully be-

Right, a seventeenth-century print of the Île de la Cité, the historic, boat-shaped island in the Seine. Settled by the Celts in pre-Roman times, it became the original nucleus of Paris. The town erected its first church to the Virgin in the sixth century.

In 1163, Louis VII (top) witnessed the laying of the cornerstone of Notre Dame by the exiled Pope Alexander III.

At his coronation in 1804, Napoleon Bonaparte (left) snatched the crown from the hands of Pope Pius VII (immediately above) and placed it on his own head. The new emperor then crowned his wife Josephine (above left).

came bishop of Paris in 1160, one of his first acts was to commission plans for a cathedral in the new style.

Parisians of all classes responded generously to Bishop Sully's call for contributions of goods and labor to the cathedral project. After centuries of stagnation, Paris was beginning to assume the stature of a national capital. The settlement on the Île de la Cité had a long history. In his *Gallic Wars,* Julius Caesar described it as a fortified town, well situated on an island in the Seine. So it remained until the mid-ninth century, when the fortifications proved no match for a decade of Viking raids. But Paris recovered and in the next 300 years grew more than it had during the previous millennium. The Chapter of Notre Dame was itself the center of a flourishing medieval university. The old cathedral, a hastily rebuilt version of a sixth-century basilica that had been burned by the Vikings, was clearly inadequate. Soon after Sully announced his plans, it was demolished unmourned, and in 1163, the exiled Pope Alexander III presided over the laying of the first stone of a new Notre Dame.

Building and decorating the new cathedral took more than 140 years, a period

during which Suger's innovative aesthetics matured into an established style. While unequivocably Gothic, the church revealed its Romanesque heritage in the round nave columns and partial four-story elevation. After his death in 1196, Bishop Sully's will provided one hundred livres, a small fortune by twelfth-century standards, for raising a lead roof. The next bishop of Paris continued with the plans of his predecessor, supervising the construction of the cathedral's western façade, which is a tripartite elevation following the design in St. Denis.

In 1218, a freak accident disrupted progress on the cathedral. When a thief from Britain attempted to steal a valuable chandelier, its burning candles ignited a tapestry and set the church ablaze. In repairing the damage, the builders altered the choir to conform to the Gothic appearance of the rest of the church. Shortly thereafter, the clerestory was heightened to admit more light, and a series of small chapels was built between the flying buttresses of the nave. A single spire, the ancestor of the present flèche, was raised in 1235 to take the place of the original belfry over the crossing.

The dominant figures during the final stages of Notre Dame's construction were not ecclesiastics but master builders and craftsmen. The rise of the Gothic coincided with increasing self-awareness. Master builders began to inscribe their

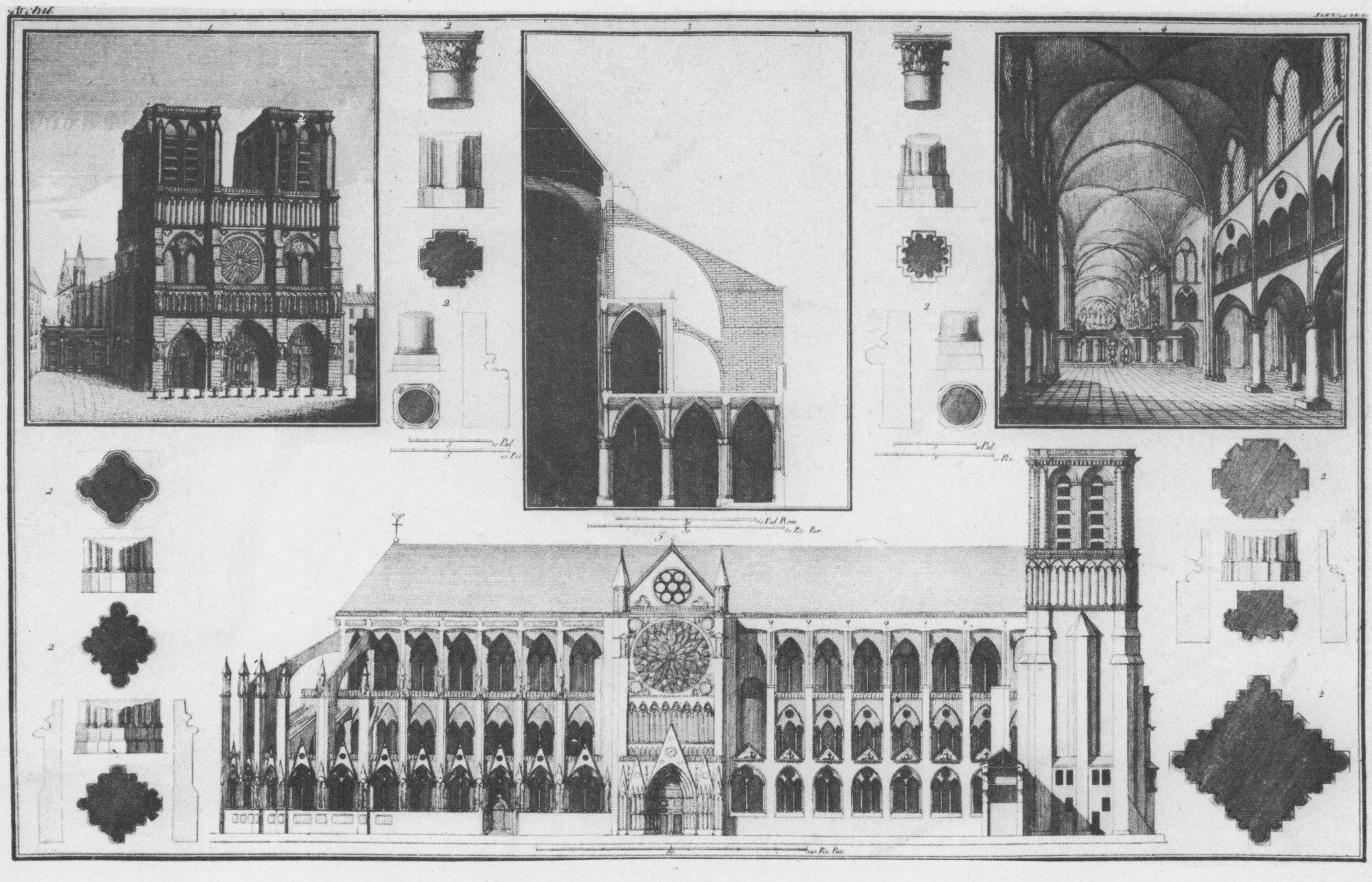

Above, architectural details of the cathedral, made before its nineteenth-century renovation. Below, the floor plan showing the original Gothic structure.

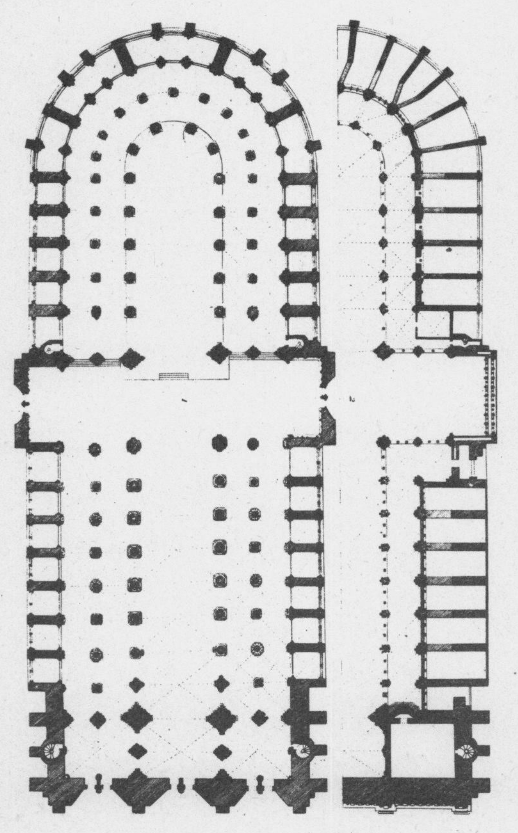

names in prominent locations on cathedral façades and floors; sculptors began to evade the restrictive rules for religious statuary by fashioning fantastic gargoyles; and glaziers refined their craft into high art. The last two masters of the cathedral were Jean de Chelles, who created the north transept with its fine rose window and began work on the south transept, and Pierre Montreuil, who completed the southern rose window during the mid-thirteenth century. De Chelles's name appears on the base of the portal of the southern transept, inscribed there by Montreuil, his successor, friend, and ardent admirer.

The inventor of the flying buttress, which first appeared at Notre Dame in about 1180 and became the cathedral's single greatest contribution to the Gothic style, remains anonymous. Some art historians believe that the first flying buttresses were created when the master builders added extra temporary supports to the regular buttresses, intending to remove them after two years or so when the mortar had settled. Later, the masons may have realized the value of the flying buttresses as a permanent support and left them in place.

The Cathedral of Notre Dame was the stage for several crucial scenes in French history. In 1214, King Philip Augustus celebrated a victory over Eleanor of Aquitaine's son King John of England by leading his army into the still-uncompleted nave for a service of thanksgiving. Twenty-five years later, the saintly Louis IX organized a quite different sort of procession, marching barefoot at the head of a parade of nobles to deposit a splinter from the true cross on a gold high altar. Notre Dame was the setting for the coronations of many kings and queens of France, including that of the English usurper Henry VI, whom Joan of Arc tried unsuccessfully to expel from French territory. And finally, in 1779, one of the last pageants of pre-Revolutionary noblesse oblige was staged here, when King Louis XVI and Marie Antoinette presided over the mass wedding of one hundred poor girls for whom they had provided dowries.

By this time, however, the architecture of Notre Dame was considered an embarrassing holdover from the barbaric, superstition-bound past. The term Gothic itself had a pejorative connotation during the Renaissance. The actual creators of Gothic art had usually referred to it simply as *opus francigenum,* or "French work." Far worse than any mere change of name were the "improvements" inflicted on the cathedral from the sixteenth through the eighteenth centuries. The gold altar was melted down and replaced by a marble one; priceless stained-glass windows were torn down and huge panels hung in their place; and as a final insult, the tympanum of the magnificent Last Judgment portal was gouged out in 1771 to create an entrance large enough for ceremonial canopies. All of these unfortunate alterations, carried out in the name of good taste and convenience, were hardly less destructive than the attack on the western façade that took place during the Revolution.

At that time, ninety sculptures were noosed by an angry mob, dragged down to the cathedral square, and decapitated. The statues represented the kings of Israel and not, as the crowd believed, the kings of France, but then religion had no more place under the Reign of Terror than royalty did. In fact, the Virgin was officially dethroned by the mob, and Notre Dame was rededicated as a temple to Reason. The scattered statue heads lay in front of the church until Jean-Baptiste Lakanal, a devout Catholic, arranged to use them as fill for his new house. Instead, Lakanal chose to respect the sacred objects and gave them a "burial." In 1977, over one and a half centuries after Lakanal's death, a routine test on the foundations of his home revealed Lakanal's secret—surveyors discovered a "grave" filled with more than twenty-five Gothic heads from Notre Dame.

Ironically, the first modern restorer of Notre Dame was Napoleon Bonaparte. Caring little for Catholicism and even less for the glories of Gothic architecture, Napoleon nevertheless realized the symbolic importance of holding his own coronation in the cathedral sanctuary. After ordering a swift renovation of the cathedral, he made his peace with the pope and with Notre Dame, sealing his treaty with the Vatican just before the observance of a high mass on Easter Sunday, 1802, over which he presided from a throne placed near the high altar.

At the beginning of the nineteenth century, taste was swinging back in the direction of romance, individualism, and fantasy. Abbot Suger's exaltation of the mystical Divine Light no longer seemed so eccentric as it had to previous generations, and intellectuals and artists began to call for the restoration of Notre Dame to its former glory. The renovation, which finally got under way in 1845, fourteen years after Victor Hugo's novel popularized the idea, was carried out by a brilliant architect named Eugène Emmanuel Viollet-le-Duc, the son of one of Napoleon's generals. Viollet-le-Duc supervised the authentic reconstruction of the façade statuary and the pointed flèche, and he made careful chemical and structural analyses of Gothic stained glass in order to reproduce as closely as possible the art of the medieval glazier. A true heir of de Chelles and Pierre Montreuil, this nineteenth-century architect even left a token signature—a statue of himself in the guise of Saint Thomas which occupies an inconspicuous place near the base of the rebuilt flèche.

Thanks to Viollet-le-Duc's efforts, Notre Dame's age is no longer held against her. Today the venerable cathedral retains its rightful place at the metaphorical and geographical heart of Paris.

Two nineteenth-century views of Notre Dame: an engraving (left) made shortly after the completion of Viollet-le-Duc's scholarly restoration; and Charles Méryon's grotesque interpretation of a gargoyle as an "insatiable vampire" (above).

Old-New Synagogue

Prague, Czechoslovakia

Preceding page, the closely packed tombstones in the Old Jewish Cemetery (on the left) and the Old-New Synagogue (on the right) in Prague, Czechoslovakia. The Baroque Jewish Town Hall (in the background) and the Old-New Synagogue are two of the few remaining landmarks of Prague's medieval Jewish quarter.

Until the eighteenth century, the law mandated that all Jews be buried inside their ghetto. Thus, some parts of the Old Cemetery (right) contain up to twelve layers of burials. Fanciful beasts and symbols of the deceased's profession or family name decorate the old tombstones. A pair of praying hands (immediately above) shows that the tomb belongs to a member of the priestly tribe of Aaron.

The gravestone of Rabbi Löw (on the opening page) is the most visited site at the cemetery. This sixteenth-century Czech mystic was known as the creator of the legendary golem, an artificial man made of clay.

Stylized carvings of a fig tree (above, below, and right) frame the main entrance to the Old-New Synagogue.

The steeply pitched roof with its dentate gables (above and detail left) is undoubtedly the synagogue's most distinctive external feature. Although the builders of medieval synagogues were heavily influenced by the Gothic style, restrictive laws and crowded ghetto conditions placed severe limitations on the architecture of Jewish houses of worship.

Many ceremonial and sacred objects belonging to Czechoslovakian Jews survived World War II because Hans Günther, a high-ranking S.S. officer in Bohemia, planned to salvage them for a postwar museum dedicated to "the culture of an extinct race." The Old-New Synagogue was preserved to become part of this museum. Among the possessions that survived the Nazi era are the gold Star of David (top left) and the synagogue's silver chandeliers (above) as well as the scrolls of the Torah (center left). Even the synagogue's medieval woodwork (right) remains intact.

Menorah candles (bottom left) illuminate a memorial to the victims of the Holocaust, found in the nearby Pinkas Synagogue. Artists worked for five years to inscribe the names and birth and death dates of 77,297 men, women, and children known to have perished at the hands of the Nazis.

שיילת

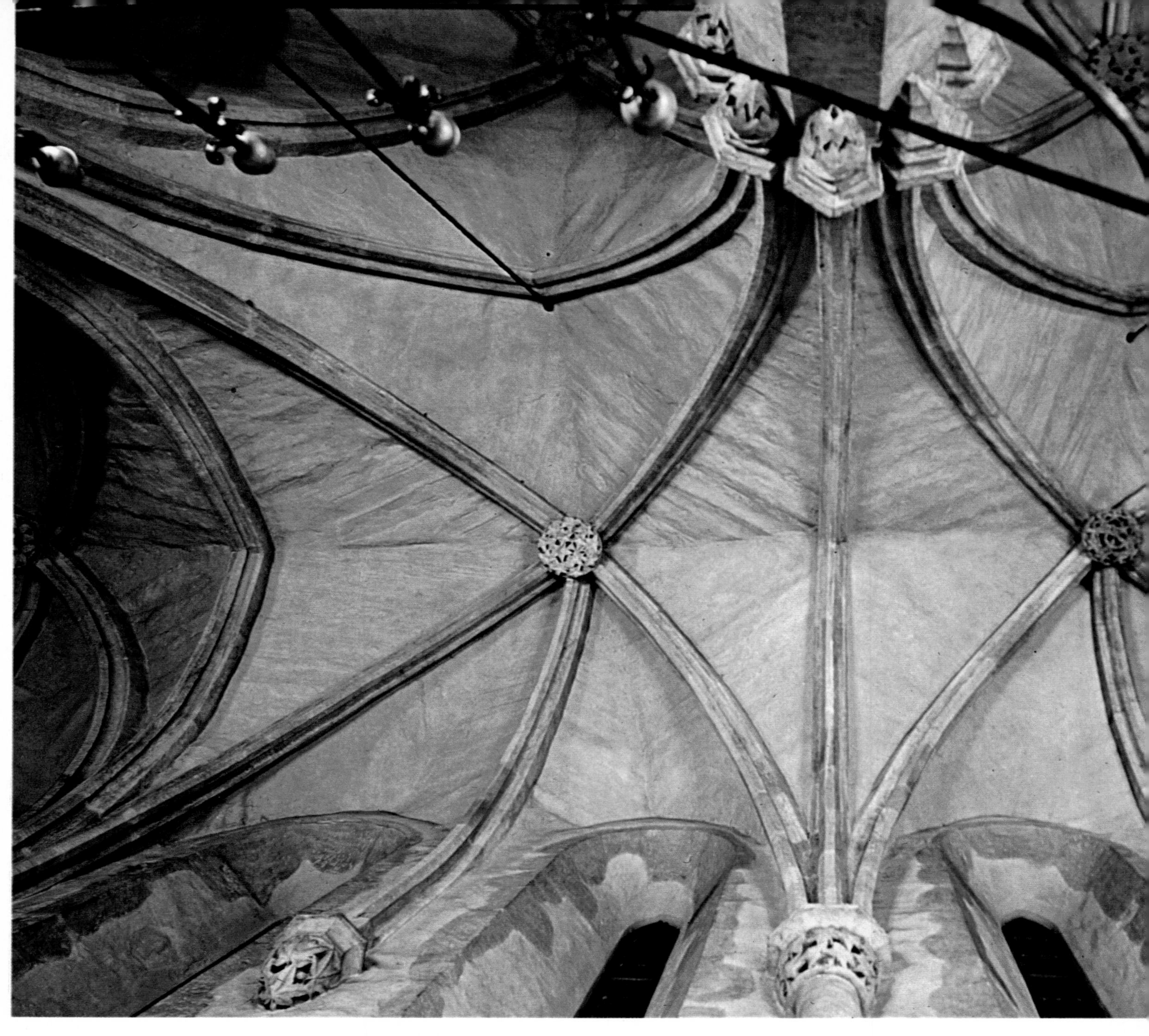

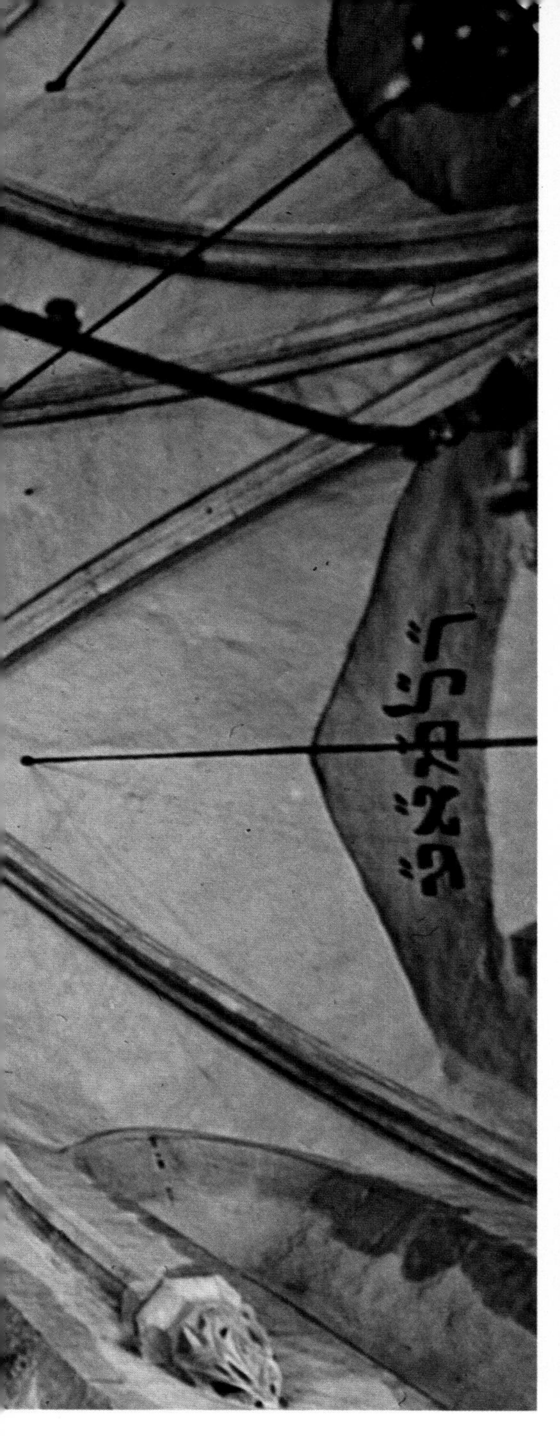

The synagogue ceiling (above left) consists of two parallel sets of ribbed vaults over the two naves—an arrangement which recalls the two-hall plan found in many German churches. These examples of carved wood tablets (near left), gilded sconces (near right), and centuries-old hangings (above right) can still be viewed in the Old-New Synagogue. Of particular interest is the banner (far left) that was presented to the Jews of Prague in 1648 by Ferdinand III in gratitude for their defense of the city against Swedish invaders.

The chair of Rabbi Löw (far right) is never used; it stands empty as a memorial to the great sixteenth-century scholar and visionary.

For hundreds of years the only trees in Prague's crowded Jewish ghetto were those which sprouted among the tombstones of Beth-Chaim, the "House of Life" cemetery (following page).

Old-New Synagogue Prague Czechoslovakia

Prague has always been a city of dreamers and visionaries, of mysteries and miracles. Its magical spirit made it the favorite haunt of Mozart. The city was also the home of Kafka, whose novels *The Trial* and *The Castle* are said to be so full of local allusions that only another native of Prague can truly understand them. The intellectual and occult traditions that mingle in this capital of old Bohemia extend to the remnants of its Jewish ghetto and the Old-New Synagogue, known as the Altenschul in German and the Staranova in Czech.

The Old-New is the oldest European synagogue still in use. For 700 years it has been the center of the Jewish community's cultural, civic, and religious activities. Nearby, in the old cemetery of Beth-Chaim, the "House of Life," lie the bodies of an estimated 200,000 Jewish men, women, and children who lived and died inside the ghetto during these seven centuries. But the part of the Old-New Synagogue that most fully captures the imagination is a small attic room which visitors may never enter. Here, it is said, lie the remains of the golem, a manlike monster fashioned of clay.

The golem was the creation of the High Rabbi Löw, a sixteenth-century religious leader who was renowned as a philosopher, mathematician, and astronomer. Rabbi Löw, a student of the Cabala, was also purported to have mystical powers. Once, when the synagogue was attacked, he is said to have transformed the stones that were thrown at him into flowers. On another occasion he invited the Emperor Rudolf II to his home, which he metamorphosed, by means of incantations, from a humble shack into an enormous mansion more magnificent than Hradčany Castle. Actually, it is highly unlikely that the Hapsburg ruler ever set foot in the ghetto, but Rudolf, who was also a student of the occult, did summon the famous rabbi to at least one midnight audience. This was an unheard of gesture in the sixteenth century, and historians and those with vivid imaginations have been speculating ever since about what the two men discussed.

Rabbi Löw's creation of the golem was his most spectacular accomplishment. The rabbi brought this clay figure to life by placing in its mouth a *shem,* or parchment, bearing the name of God. The golem worked all week as the rabbi's servant and protector, dutifully performing whatever tasks the rabbi assigned to him. But on one Sabbath, the rabbi was too busy to remember to remove the shem as he usually did. At sundown the golem ran amuck. As flames leaped from his eyes, he destroyed everything in his path, knocking over a section of the synagogue wall and uprooting trees. After this display, the congrega-

The medieval synagogue was the center of civic as well as religious life. This seventeenth-century drawing by the Dutch artist Moeyart shows the men of a Jewish community assembled for a reading and discussion of the sacred scriptures.

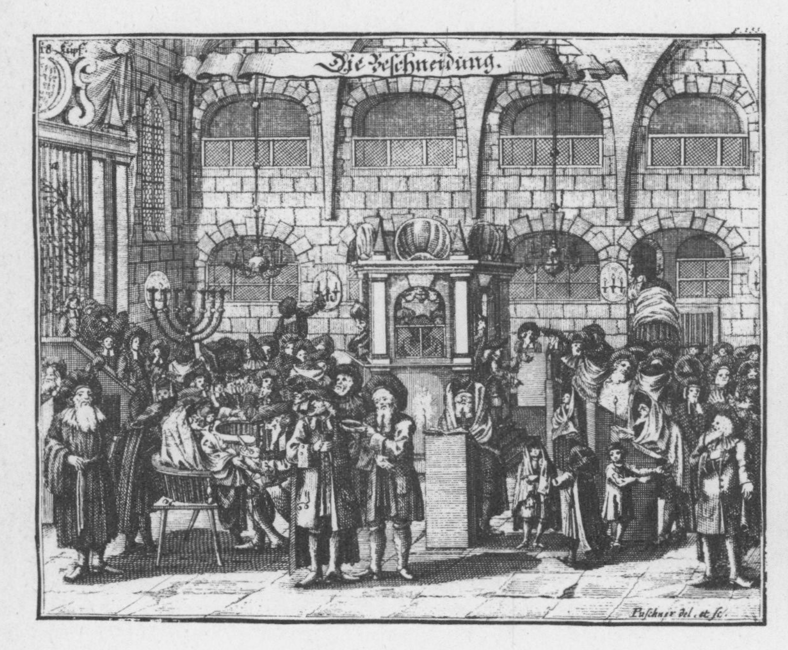

Above, scenes from medieval Jewish rituals as depicted in an old German book (left to right): a circumcision, a commemoration of the destruction of Jerusalem, a wedding, and a burial within the ghetto walls.

tion begged Rabbi Löw to destroy the monster, so he removed the shem for the final time, rendering the golem lifeless forever.

This is only one version of the legend. Others say that the creature, sometimes given the name Joseph Golem, sealed his doom when he fell in love with the rabbi's daughter or, alternatively, that the Emperor Rudolf agreed to call off an impending pogrom in exchange for Rabbi Löw's promise to destroy his creation. In any case, clay fragments of the golem are supposed to be stored away in the attic room of the Old-New Synagogue where Rabbi Löw secretively performed his occult experiments.

The story of the golem is known throughout the world, but it is just one of many legends treasured by the Jewish community of Prague. When the elders of the community gathered in the year A.D. 925 to lay the foundations of the Old-New Synagogue, they were said to have discovered stones from the Temple of Jerusalem buried at the building site. These stones, it seems, had been carried to Prague by exiles who fled the Holy City after the destruction of the temple by the Roman Emperor Vespasian in A.D. 70. According to this story, the synagogue's true name is not Altenschul but Altenai-Schul, from a Hebrew phrase that means literally the "on-condition-that synagogue." The building was so named because two visiting wise men from Jerusalem—some say they were angels—warned the Jews of Prague that they could use the temple stones only "on condition that" they would be returned to the Holy City when the Messiah appeared.

Notwithstanding this miraculous tale, most scholars place the founding of the Old-New Synagogue in about the year 1270. By this time, the tolerant mood of the twelfth century—when Central European Jews and Christians joined forces against their pagan enemies—was no more than a memory. The ghetto had become a closed world that Jews could not escape, even in death. Forbidden to expand for any reason, the Jewish quarter became dreadfully crowded, and the cemetery was the most crowded place of all. When every available grave site was filled, there was nothing to do but begin again. In some parts of the Beth-Chaim cemetery, burials extend twelve layers below the present ground level. Some 10,000 tombstones still exist above ground, the oldest bearing the date 1438.

Hebrew tradition dictated that synagogues be built in a prominent place with their doors facing east. But there were no prominent open spaces in the Prague ghetto. Synagogues were also supposed to be tall. But government regulations specified that Jewish places of worship in Prague be small and inconspicuous. At the same time, the builders of medieval synagogues were, naturally enough, influenced by the splendors of Gothic architecture, and the Old-New Synagogue is firmly rooted in the tradition of Czech Gothic church architecture.

There were, of course, modifications. Because the Jews were not permitted to build anything that would compete with the tall churches of Prague, they settled for stocky, truncated exterior buttresses and a steeply pitched, brick gable that was typically late Gothic. The double-nave plan of the interior and the five-ribbed, pointed ceiling vaults were also typical of many German churches of the time. Guidebooks to the synagogue often state that the fifth rib of the vault was added to avoid the Christian overtones of the more common four-rib pattern. This may be a true explanation. Many late Gothic churches, however, have five-ribbed vaults, and as the building trades were forbidden to Jews during this period, there is a strong possibility that the design was chosen as a matter of course by Christian masons.

The exterior of the synagogue has been altered twice: once in 1536 and again in

1754, when the building was probably first called the Old-New. The interior, however, consists of the original medieval structure. Although the building is small in comparison with Gothic cathedrals, its interior space is much greater than one would expect. This is because the floor is well below street level—a strategy for circumventing the height restrictions. At the center of the sanctuary stands the bema, a raised platform which originally held the sacred Ark containing the scrolls of the Torah. In accordance with an early custom, the bema was also furnished with a chair, called the Seat of Moses, and a draped desk where the rabbi sat for readings of the Torah. Women were not permitted in the naves but could observe religious ceremonies from an adjoining alcove by peering through slits in the wall. Today, the Orthodox practice of separating the sexes is still followed. The Ark, however, has been moved to a somewhat more visible position against the western wall of the synagogue. The Seat of Moses, said to have been used by Rabbi Löw, also stands along this wall. Out of respect for this great leader, it remains perpetually empty.

The survival of so many of the synagogue's furnishings and ritual objects is remarkable in view of the long and troubled history of the Prague ghetto. Apparently, the serene, almost antiseptic interior that remains today bears little resemblance to the appearance of the

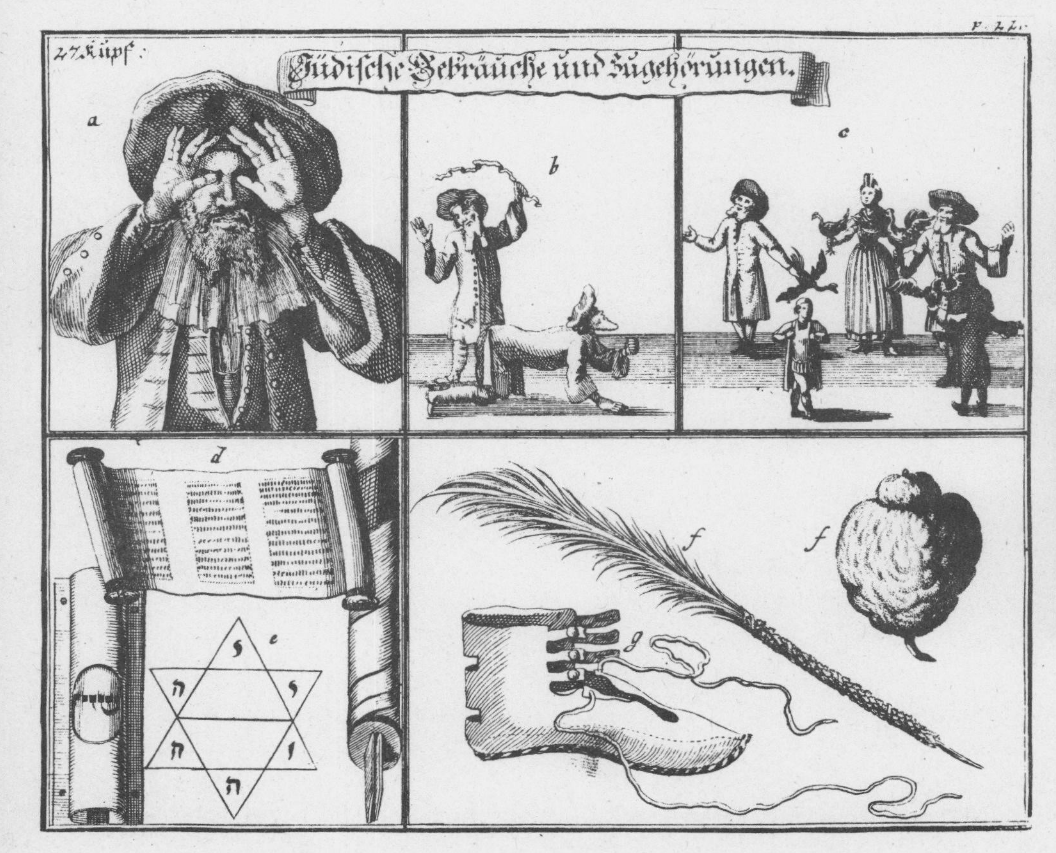

Left, illustrations from an old German manuscript showing Jewish rituals and religious articles and symbols. Above, an illuminated marriage certificate with a highly stylized depiction of the newly-wed couple.

Left, a painting by Edward Krem, dated 1892, showing the Old-New Synagogue ringed by buildings of the ghetto quarter. Four years later the ghetto was torn down, with the exception of a few landmarks that were preserved as historical monuments.

Left, an old illustration depicting the synagogue's high, ribbed vaults and the seats that line both the exterior walls and those around the bema in the center.

synagogue when it was in much heavier use. Hans Christian Andersen, who visited the Old-New in 1866, reported that the interior was "black with soot, and there was such a terrible stench of onions that I had to get out in the open air." But there are other stains, symbolic if not literal, that can never be effaced. In 1389, during a pogrom, rioters pursued the rabbis and elders of Prague into the synagogue and slit their throats on the steps of the bema. Prague Jews still point to dark blotches on the synagogue walls that are said to be the blood of these martyrs.

The pogrom of 1389 was among the more violent episodes in a long history of persecutions. One of Prague's most bizarre landmarks is a crucifix, inscribed with large Hebrew letters, that stands on the Charles Bridge, evidence of another and more typical form of discrimination. It was erected and paid for by the ghetto as a collective punishment after one Prague Jew was accused of desecrating a crucifix.

In spite of the persecutions, the Prague ghetto was largely autonomous until 1848, when it became a flourishing center of rabbinical scholarship. And by the early decades of the twentieth century, Prague was the home of the most free and culturally advanced Jewish community in Eastern Europe. Ironically enough, this prosperity rested on the close linguistic and cultural ties that had grown up between the Jews and Prague's German-speaking elite.

Of course, when the Nazis entered Prague, this connection with the German community availed the Jews nothing. Of the 360,000 Jews in Czechoslovakia in 1939, only 42,000 survived World War II and half of these later emigrated. The names of over 77,000 victims of Nazism have been inscribed as a memorial on the walls of the Pinkas Synagogue, a much smaller structure that stands across from the Old-New on the far side of the Beth-Chaim cemetery.

The Pinkas Synagogue, long attributed to a sixteenth-century architect and used as the private *schul* (synagogue) of a wealthy ghetto family, is actually older than the Old-New Synagogue. Nevertheless, it was to the Old-New that the 8,000 Prague Jews who survived the Holocaust returned. Today, despite the ambivalent attitude of the Czechoslovakian government, which has sponsored memorials to the victims of Nazism while banning Zionist activity, there are again regular services in the Old-New Synagogue. And if Prague no longer seems the city of miracles that it once was, there are still a few old residents who claim that they have seen the golem emerge from his attic room at midnight to tend the nearby grave of Rabbi Löw.

Melk Monastery

Austria

The ancient abbey of Melk, forty-four miles west of Vienna on the Danube, dominates the city and the surrounding landscape. Founded in the tenth century by the Babenberg dynasty of Austria, the abbey was rebuilt in the late Baroque style by Jakob Prandtauer, who brilliantly accommodated the building to the contours of the promontory it so dramatically occupies (preceding page).

Above left, the monastery as seen from the northwest. Left, the irregularly laid-out residential quarters of the Benedictine monks at Melk. The abbey church rises impressively above flanking wings containing the Marmorsaal, or Marble Hall, and the library (above right). The façade of the church (right) is framed by a pair of sculptural towers that terminates in ornate and bulbous cupolas, executed by Joseph Munggenast after the originals were destroyed by fire.

The Melk complex is reached by an eastern entrance that leads to a small outer courtyard. Above, the main façade, with its graceful pilasters, as seen from the outer courtyard. The larger inner courtyard, known as the Prelates' Court, can be glimpsed through the portico known as the Benediktihallè. Left, a view from the Prelates' Court back toward the outer court. Right, the playful ornamental fountain of the Prelates' Court.

These pages, views of the Prelates' Court. The delicate Rococo dome of the church rises elegantly above the western end (above right). Below far right, the entrance side of the Prelates' Court. The courtyard façades, modulated by simple pilasters, are subtly bound together by the horizontal white and yellow "rustications" of the ground floor and the string-course of the main floor. The focal point of the court is the elaborate fountain in its decoratively shaped pool (above).

Peter and Paul (below near right) guard the "keys of the kingdom" on a blue and gilt medallion above the eastern arch of the Benediktihalle.

The buildings of the western part of the monastery are grouped closely together on the narrowing ridge. On three sides, the church either directly abuts the surrounding buildings or is separated from them by narrow shadowy arcades (left and below).

Facing page, the top-floor corridor of the extremely long south wing, the Emperor's Gallery, which is lined with royal portraits. Light pours in from the row of fifty-nine windows in the lengthy unbroken façade. It is occupied by apartments that were frequently used by Hapsburg visitors.

The interior of the church, though based on a simple and forceful design, is a characteristically Baroque explosion of ornamental effects. Like many Austrian buildings of the period, it was decorated by Italian artists—among them Gaetano Fanti, Antonio Bibiena, and the sculptor Lorenzo Matielli—under the supervision of the theatrical designer Antonio Beduzzi. Left, the organ loft over the entrance to the nave, as seen from the main altar. The ceiling of the transverse barrel vaults was frescoed by Johann Michael Rottmayr. The wealth of decorative effects is restrained and organized by Prandtauer's great molded entablature, which magnificently defines the border between walls and vaults.

Above, the nave and main altar. The clerestory windows and dome provide a rich, subtle illumination. The dome, resting on frescoed pendentives, also contributes a sense of height and expansiveness, an effect that is crucial to all pilgrimage churches.

Right, a radiant gilt gloria in the transept above the altar and sarcophagus of Saint Coloman, one of the patron saints of Melk. The Biblical text above reads: "The righteous man shall flourish like the palm tree" (Psalms 91:13).

Above, the former high altar (the main altar has now been placed under the dome). The setting appears almost theatrical, with Peter and Paul in the center of the stage, surrounded by gesticulating supporting characters. Designed by Lorenzo Matielli and executed by the Austrian sculptor Peter Widerin, the gilt figures are complemented by the pinkish-ocher tone of the marble and stucco setting designed by Prandtauer.

Center right, the organ, built in 1732 by Gottfried Sonnholz. Music-making cherubs and angels are fancifully perched on the pipes.

Far right, top and bottom, the dome and transverse barrel vaults of the nave, with frescoes by Johann Michael Rottmayr. Center far right, the ceiling of the summer sacristy, Rottmayr's trial piece for the church ceiling. This sacristy was completed in 1703, and services were held here during the rest of the construction.

CON
STANTIA
ET
FORTITV
DINE.

The staircase (left and below), with its white stucco arabesques, links the floors of the southern guest wing. Completed in 1716, it is acclaimed for its delicate ceilings and the sculpture group by Matielli on an upper landing, honoring the new Emperor Charles VI.

Above, the Marmorsaal, the marble reception hall at the western end of the guest wing. The simple gray and pink are enlivened by the black pilaster capitals—torsos of Moors framed in gilt. The room is horizontally defined by inlaid plinths below the pilasters. A bold entablature above is ingeniously continued in Gaetano Fanti's painted balustrade, which borders Paul Troger's ceiling fresco of Humanity Led by Reason.

Above, a salon of the imperial apartments in the guest wing, with an ornate Rococo room stove of gilded white majolica in one corner. Although most of the present furnishings date from the nineteenth century, these sumptuous apartments still boast intricately stuccoed ceilings and treasures, such as the paintings that can be glimpsed through the door and the marble crucifix (left).

Most of the art treasures at Melk are in the archives of the library wing (below), which is across the western courtyard from the Marmorsaal. They include a jeweled gold reliquary of the jaw of Saint Coloman (above) and the gold Cross of Melk (below right). Embellished with gems and filigree, the cross was presented to the abbey around 1360 by the Hapsburg Duke Rudolf IV and contains a fragment of the true cross.

Right, part of the picture collection housed in the Prälatur, the building at the western end of the Prelates' Court, whose trompe l'oeil ceiling fresco was painted by the Italian artist Hippolyto Sconzani.

Above and below, the spiral staircases with wrought-iron banisters within the towers of the church. The stairs lead from the upper floors of the library and the Marmorsaal into the main floor of the contiguous church. The underside of the stairs is frescoed in traditional motifs, such as acanthus leaves and egg-and-dart moldings (right).

Facing page, the library of Melk, which contains 75,000 printed volumes, 1,800 manuscripts, and 800 incunabula (early printed books). Bookcases line the walls of the main hall (above right), whose upper levels are reached by the scroll-supported wooden balcony. As in the Marmorsaal, the painted entablature above is the work of Gaetano Fanti.

The gilded details and book bindings (below, left to right) highlight the restrained warmth of the woodwork and play an integral part in the harmonious decoration of the room. The illusionistically painted entrance, which gives an impression of three dimensions, leads to the staircase (left).

Above, one of the gilded wood figures of the four Faculties *(Divisions of Learning) by Joseph Pöbl on the main door of the hall.*

Melk Monastery Austria

Had he been any more experienced, Jakob Prandtauer might have wondered if he were equal to the undertaking. On April 6, 1702, this provincial builder from St. Pölten in Lower Austria was handed a task that would have intimidated the most seasoned of architects: He was to rebuild the Benedictine abbey at Melk on its isolated site 180 feet above the Danube. This hilltop structure, reputed to be the largest monastic edifice in the world, survives as a testimony to his vision, one that he felt "bound to answer for before God and honest men."

The abbey has a commanding position on a narrow, wedge-shaped ridge that falls away steeply toward the river. Naturally adapted to defense, the site was originally a Roman garrison, later gaining prominence when it became the first home of the Babenbergs, the Austrian ruling house from the tenth to the thirteenth centuries.

In the late tenth century, the Babenberg Margrave Leopold I turned over the castle on the site to a community of lay canons and established a church in honor of Peter and Paul. Then, in 1089, Leopold II replaced the lay canons with a community of Benedictine monks. The order, famous for its remarkable collection of books, sacred relics, and wine, endures to this day. In 1113, Leopold III, who endowed several monasteries in Austria, gave over the Melk site to the monks in perpetuity, along with rich neighboring landholdings. Leopold's practice of establishing Austrian monasteries earned him a canonization in 1485.

During the Hapsburg wars of the fourteenth century, a bastion was added to the great complex of residential and administrative buildings. As if this mixture of roles were not enough, Melk was also a celebrated center of learning and teaching,

Below, an engraving of 1638 from the archives of the Benedictine abbey of Melk, founded in the eleventh century. The walled complex shown here displays many of the features of the present monastery, but without the unity and logic of Jakob Prandtauer's design (1702). The close collaboration between Prandtauer and Abbot Dietmayr at a particularly flourishing time in Melk's history produced what has been called the finest of all late Baroque monasteries.

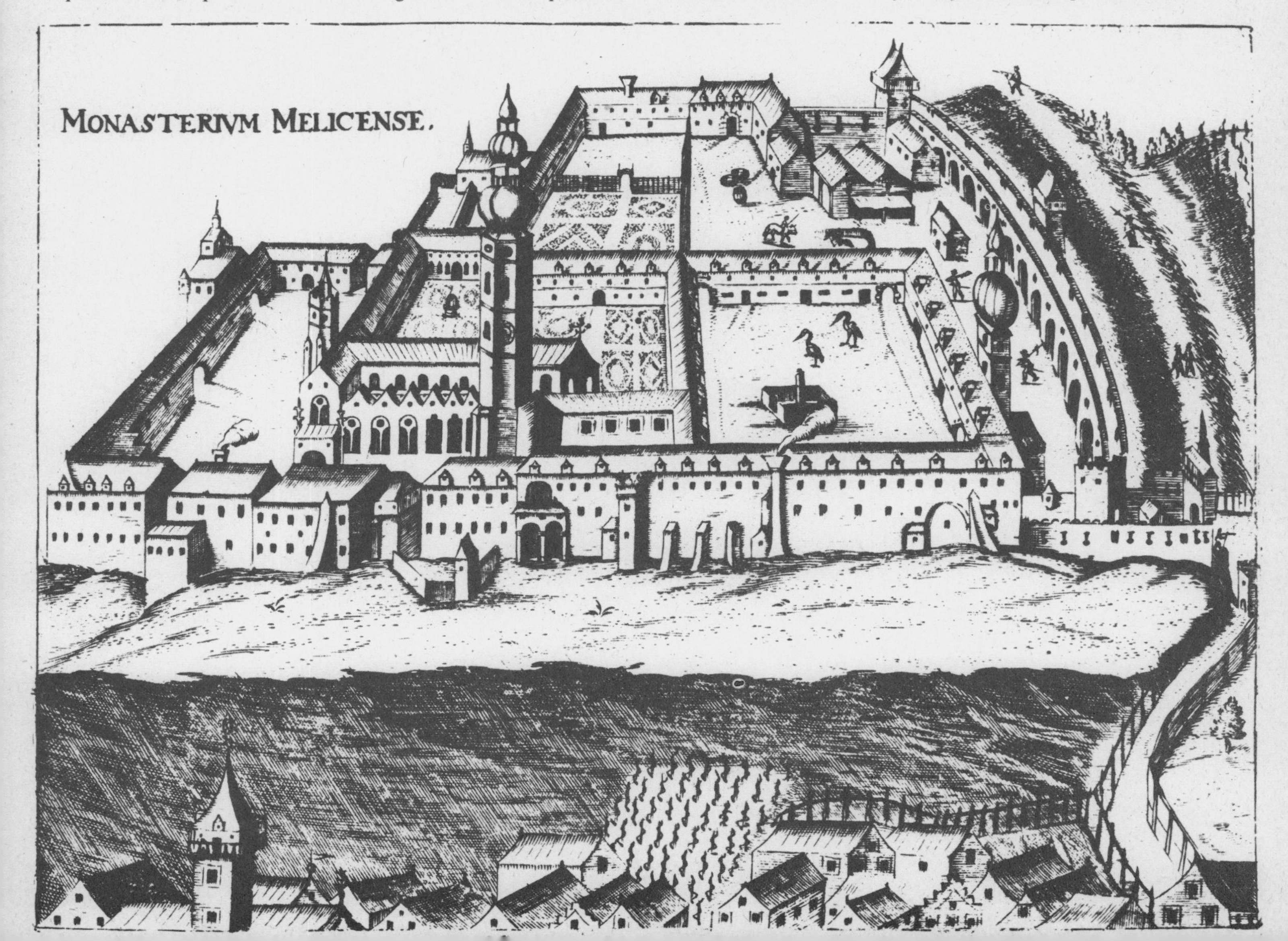

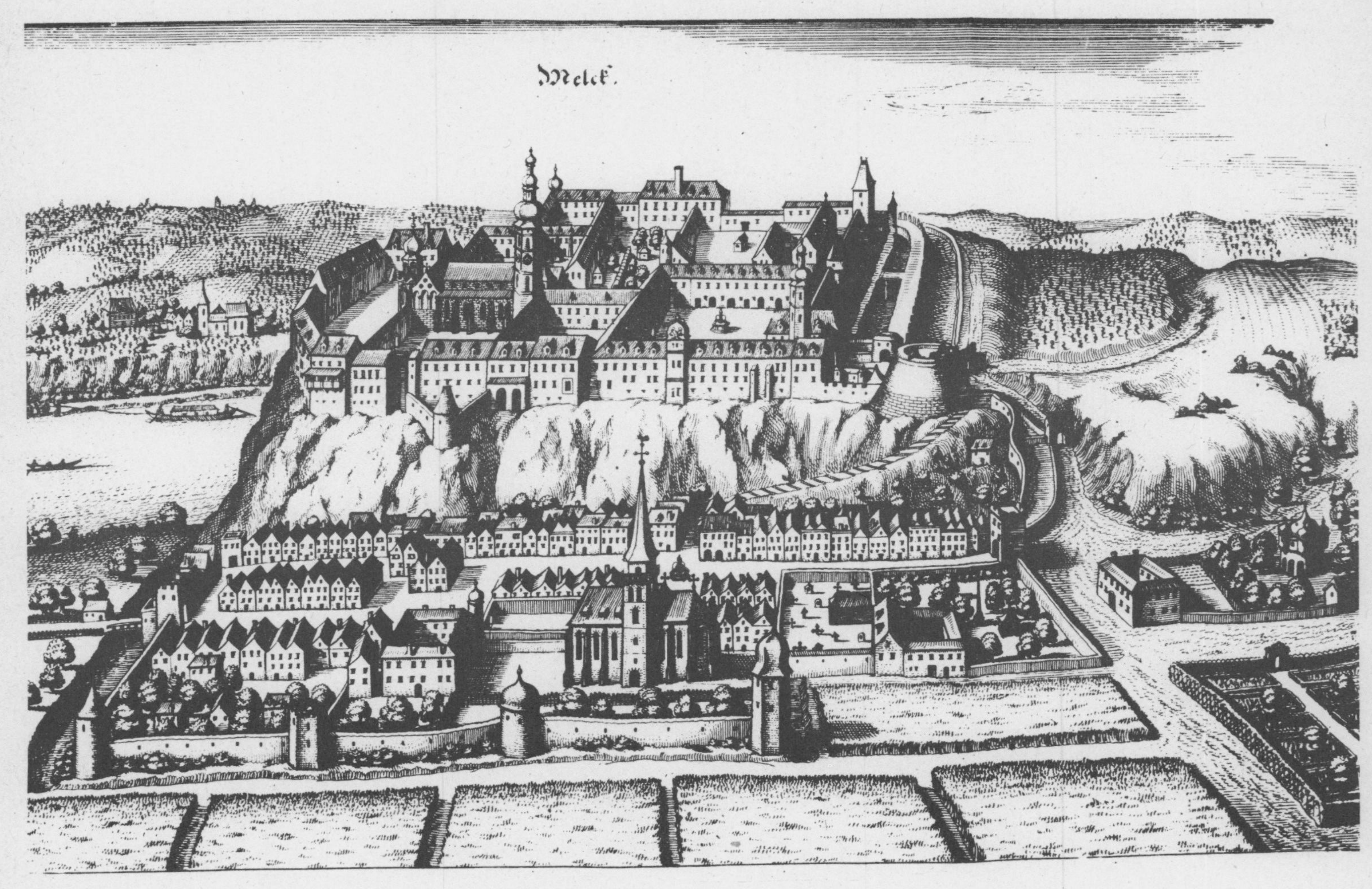

Above, a seventeenth-century engraving of the monastery and the town of Melk below. The neat row of houses lining the rocky hillside can still be seen today.

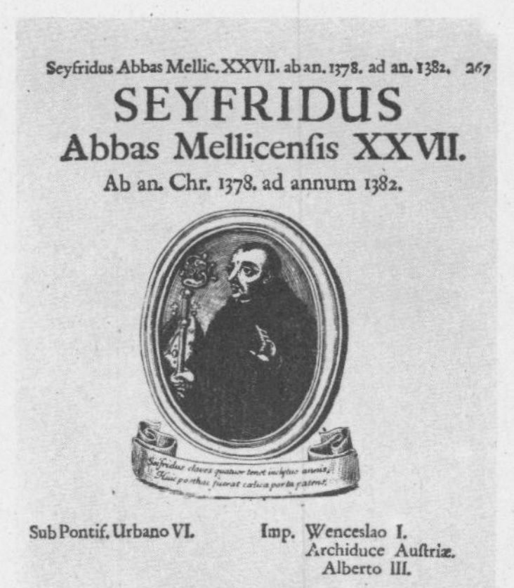
Seyfridus Abbas Mellic. XXVII. ab an. 1378. ad an. 1382. 267

SEYFRIDUS
Abbas Mellicenſis XXVII.
Ab an. Chr. 1378. ad annum 1382.

Sub Pontif. Urbano VI. Imp. Wenceslao I.
Archiduce Auſtriæ.
Alberto III.

278 Chronici Mellicenſis Pars IV.

LUDOVICUS II.
Abbas Mellicenſis XXXIX.
Ab an. Chr. 1387. uſque ad an. 1410.

Sub P. Pontif. Urbano VI. I. Imp. Wenceslao.
Bonifacio IX. Ruperto.
Innocentio VII. Archiducibus Auſtriæ.
Gregorio XII. Alberto III.
Alexandro V. Alberto IV. &
Joanne XXIII. Alberto V.

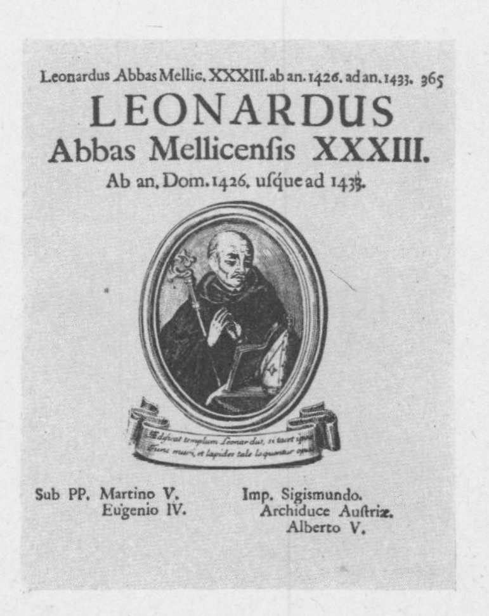
Leonardus Abbas Mellic. XXXIII. ab an. 1426. ad an. 1433. 365

LEONARDUS
Abbas Mellicenſis XXXIII.
Ab an. Dom. 1426. uſque ad 1433.

Sub PP. Martino V. Imp. Sigismundo.
Eugenio IV. Archiduce Auſtriæ.
Alberto V.

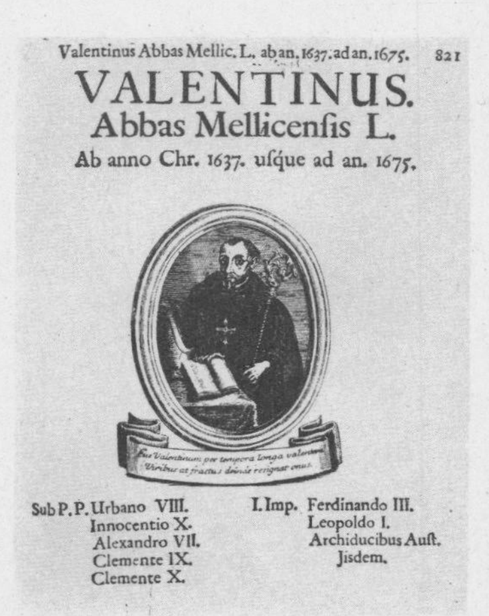
Valentinus Abbas Mellic. L. ab an. 1637. ad an. 1675. 821

VALENTINUS.
Abbas Mellicenſis L.
Ab anno Chr. 1637. uſque ad an. 1675.

Sub P. P. Urbano VIII. I. Imp. Ferdinando III.
Innocentio X. Leopoldo I.
Alexandro VII. Archiducibus Auſt.
Clemente IX. Jisdem.
Clemente X.

Left, title pages from volumes of the abbey chronicle, the Chronicon Mellicense, *in the edition published by the distinguished historian and member of the Melk brotherhood, Anselm Schramb. It first appeared in 1702 on the eve of the great rebuilding project. The chronicle contains an early plan of the church by Prandtauer.*

with extensive scholarly facilities as well as an excellent convent school. Moreover, the monastery was frequently obliged to offer hospitality to clergymen of the province, members of associated Benedictine convents, and members of the imperial family. The Hapsburgs often used the regional monasteries as temporary lodgings, thus making themselves less dependent upon the landed nobility.

Although the monastery escaped relatively unscathed from the Turkish wars of the sixteenth and seventeenth centuries, it was devastated by a fire in 1683 during which the monks ingeniously but ineffectually cast wine on the flames after the water ran out. Piecemeal reconstructions might have gone on indefinitely had not the great Benedictine monasteries been caught up in the passion for building which descended on a newly prosperous Austria after the expulsion of the Turks in 1683. This enthusiasm was personified at Melk by Berthold Dietmayr, who became abbot in 1700 at the age of thirty.

Like many young men in Lower Austria, Dietmayr received his early education at the convent school of Melk. He then entered the monastery itself in 1687 as a monk. He was to develop strong ties with the metropolis of Vienna which, in the last century of the Holy Roman Empire, was enjoying its role as one of the great cosmopolitan capitals of Europe. In addition to acting as spokesman for the prelatic *Stand* (estate) in the Lower Austrian provincial diet, Dietmayr was a councilor at the courts of the emperors Joseph I and Charles VI. In 1706, he became rector of the University of Vienna, where he had once undertaken higher studies. Considering his entrenchment in imperial circles, Dietmayr could have easily commissioned one of the most fashionable Viennese architects of the day to carry out the immense rebuilding program which he had conceived for Melk. Instead he chose Jakob Prandtauer, a builder with no more than a local reputation.

Dietmayr's choice was a daring one. At the time he was chosen, Prandtauer was an ex-sculptor in his early forties with a stronger theoretical than practical background in the field of architecture. A stonemason's son from the Tyrol region of Austria, Prandtauer had traveled throughout southern Germany during his youth and acquired a thorough knowledge of German and Italian architecture. Unlike his contemporaries Johann Fischer von Erlach and Lucas von Hildebrandt, he was content to be known as *Baumeister* (master builder) or even *Mauermeister* (master mason) rather than by the grander name of *Architekt*. The construction of Melk, spanning his entire building career, was his first important undertaking and the crowning achievement of his life.

Prandtauer succeeded not only in crowding an enormously diversified set of buildings onto the restricted, asymmetrical space on the ridge, but also in conferring an easily recognizable order and logic on the arrangement. The coherence of the design is remarkable considering that by the time the last artisan had left the site in 1749—after a dozen years of construction, followed by thirty more years spent in decorating the building—both Prandtauer and Abbot Dietmayr had long since died. Indeed, the Benedictines at Melk must have forgotten what it was like to live without disruption.

The progress of the work is well documented in the records of the abbey archives. Demolition of the old buildings

The Turkish invasion of Austria, which brought the Ottoman army to the walls of Vienna in 1683, inspired this anonymous representation of Saint Benedict leading the Austrian army in defense of Melk's monastery (below). Although the Benedictine abbey escaped major destruction during the Turkish wars, a fire in 1683 devastated most of the complex, necessitating extensive reconstruction.

Above left, a portrait of Jakob Prandtauer which now hangs at the entrance to the Marmorsaal. It depicts the architect in vigorous middle age, standing at the entrance to the Prelates' Court.

Above right, an engraving of Berthold Dietmayr, the energetic abbot who initiated the rebuilding of the monastery during the eighteenth century. Below, two manuscripts from the great collection of the Melk library, recording some of the early Babenberg endowments to the monastery.

and construction of the new proceeded in stages so that the regular functions of the community could be moved into various makeshift arrangements. Prandtauer was instructed to build on the old foundations wherever he could and to incorporate any salvageable structures.

Construction began in 1702 with what is now the summer sacristy of the church, where temporary services were first held in 1703. The team of artists and artisans included the Italian theatrical designer Antonio Beduzzi, the Italian sculptor Lorenzo Matielli, and the painter Johann Michael Rottmayr. But Prandtauer's authority appears to have been final in every detail, even down to the supervision of deliveries.

The architect's plans, scale drawings, and models were copious and remarkably detailed. The documentation was so complete that, after Prandtauer's death in 1726, Abbot Dietmayr proposed to use them to carry on the work himself with no other supervision save that of Prandtauer's foreman. But the attempt to continue without an architect proved unsuccessful. In 1729, Prandtauer's cousin and pupil Joseph Munggenast was employed to complete the work according to his predecessor's design. By the time of Munggenast's death in 1741, only the finishing touches remained. These would take an additional eight years to accomplish.

Munggenast's chief original contributions were a domed pavilion in the once-elegant formal gardens north of the monastery walls and the famous elaborate bell towers that flank the façade of the church. The simpler towers built in the same place by Prandtauer had been destroyed by fire in 1738.

The monastery at Melk seems to perch precariously on its dramatic hilltop site. Seen from the Danube below, it towers straight out of the cliff; seen from the entrance at the opposite end, it has a more sedate, evenly graduated appearance, starting with the two great bulwarks that border the gate. Prandtauer added a bulwark of his own to the surviving earlier structure. Between these dissimilar ends of the monastery, the complex is arranged with unobtrusive asymmetry—the result of the contours of the site and the use of the existing foundations. The guest wing on the southeast side has a single, unbroken façade, about 1,050 feet long, while the northwest side is an irregular, staggered progression of wings built on the medieval foundations. This asymmetry is not noticeable from either within the complex or

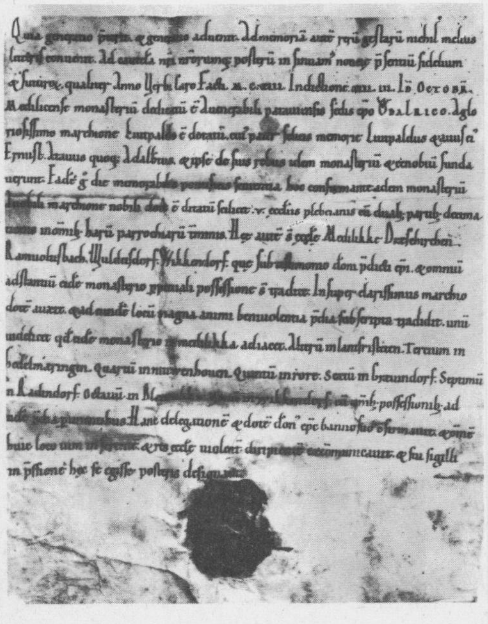

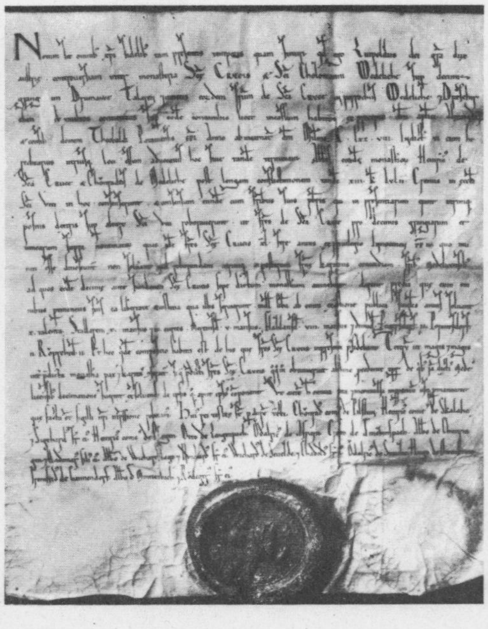

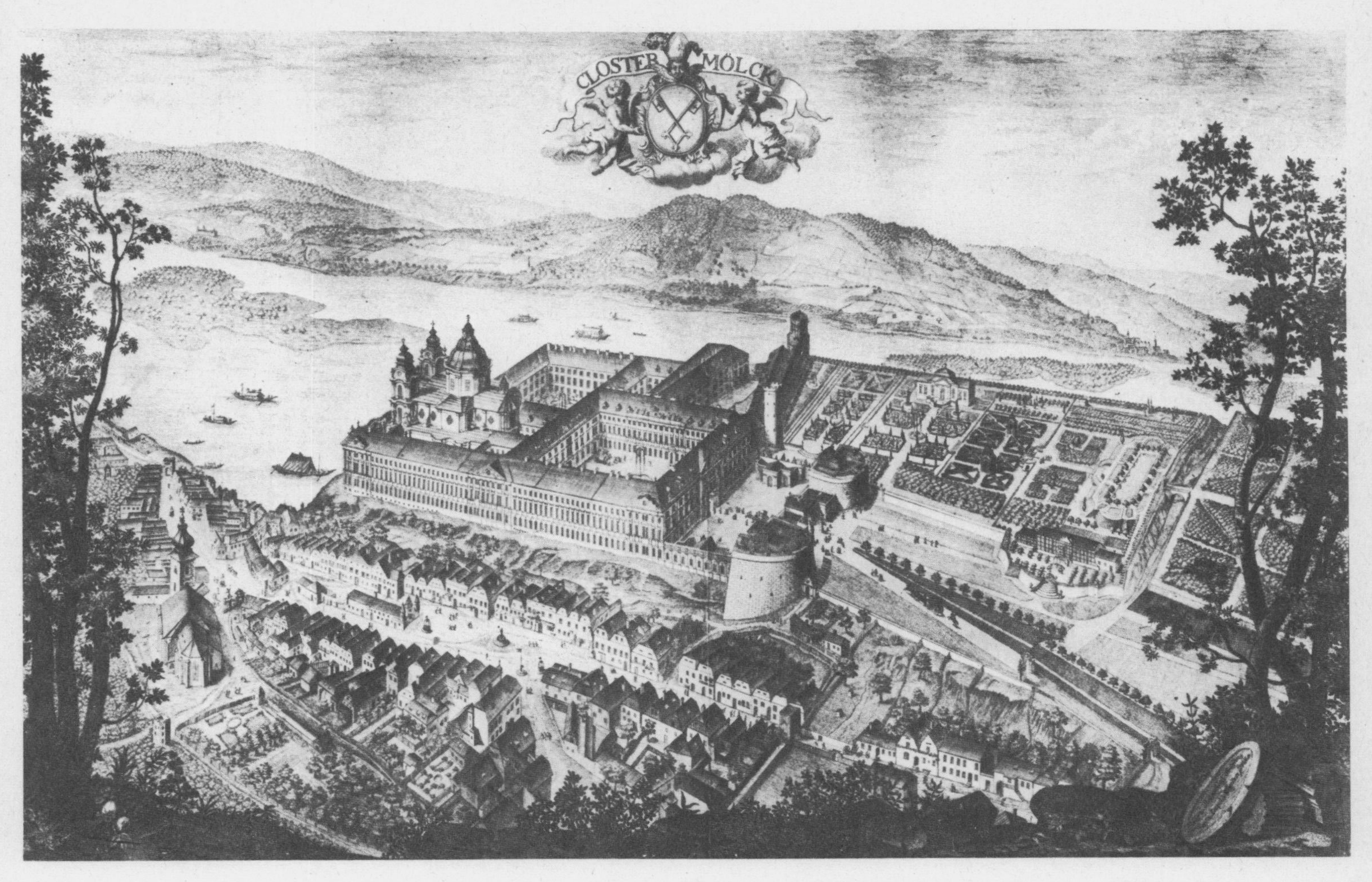

Above, an eighteenth-century representation of the monastery in Melk after its reconstruction by Jakob Prandtauer. Today the abbey appears as it was two centuries ago, although the extensive formal gardens to the north no longer exist. Melk is still a spectacular sight for travelers approaching the city from the Danube.

the town below.

The north approach to the monastery is guarded by the two curved bastions that flank a gate house framed by two pillars. These columns, the work of Lorenzo Matielli, bear statues of Saint Leopold and Saint Coloman. The story behind Coloman's sainthood is unlikely but intriguing. In the late tenth century, this young man—said to be the son of a king of Ireland—was traveling in Austria as an anonymous pilgrim on his way to the Holy Land. On July 16, 1012, he was arrested as a spy. The next day he was tortured and then hanged. Two years later, after a series of miracles were reported to have occurred at Coloman's burial site, the Margrave Henry I had the body transferred to Melk. Saint Coloman was made patron saint of Austria, a distinction he held until he was superseded by Saint Leopold III in 1663. He remains the national protector of two dissimilar groups: farm animals and marriageable women.

Beyond the gate house and an outer courtyard stands the eastern façade of the monastery complex. It has a surface of white marble and light yellow stucco, crowned by a pediment bearing the words *Absit gloriari nisi in cruce* ("Let there be no glorying except in the Cross," Galatians 6:14). Above the inscription is a cross copied from one of the treasures in the archives of the monastery. An arched opening, flanked by obelisks and statues of Peter and Paul, leads to a deep-vaulted portico known as the Benediktihalle.

Through the portico lies the spacious Prelates' Court which stretches 273 by 136 feet. Beyond this courtyard rises the massive, sixteen-sided church dome. A more modest version of the façades of the outer court is continued on all the sides within. These feature the horizontal white and yellow rustications and moldings on the ground-level "basement," simple pilasters that do not interrupt the regular rhythm of the pediment-topped windows, and balustradelike parapets.

The courtyard is enclosed by part of the guest wing on the left and the residential buildings on the right. In the center stands the eastern façade of the Prälatur, or Prelacy. Here the abbots of Melk once entertained ecclesiastical guests. Today it houses a fine collection of paintings. From within the courtyard, the eye is first drawn not to the enclosing façades but to the copper-roofed dome of the church behind the Prelacy and to its reflection in the pool of the courtyard fountain. The dome takes the shape of a bell, its outline subtly broken up into shallow upper and lower S curves. The whole pattern is repeated in miniature on the delicate lantern above it.

The interior of the guest wing consists of a long set of corridors—660 feet—illuminated on one side by the windows of the southeast façade. The doors of the imperial apartments open off the other side. On the top floor is the celebrated Emperor's Gallery, hung with portraits of all the Austrian sovereigns beginning with Leopold I of Babenberg. Below the gallery, Prandtauer's dignified staircase, with its vaulted roof traced with delicate stucco work, leads to an imposing group of allegorical figures by Matielli. They commemorate the motto of Charles VI, who was emperor at the time of the construction of the wing: *Constantia et fortitudine* ("By constancy and strength").

At the far end of the guest wing is the lofty reception hall known as the Marmorsaal, or Marble Hall. Off the Marmorsaal is a curved balcony which approximates the limits of the cliff contours and swings around the cliff to connect with the monastery's famous library. As of the last decade, Melk's library contained 75,000 volumes and 1,800 manuscripts, dating from the ninth century. The most remarkable pieces of the collection are said to be two Gutenberg Bibles. The abbey originally had a third Gutenberg Bible, but it was purchased by the Library of Congress in Washington, D.C., for the diplomatic sum of one million dollars. The problem of heating this spacious library was neatly

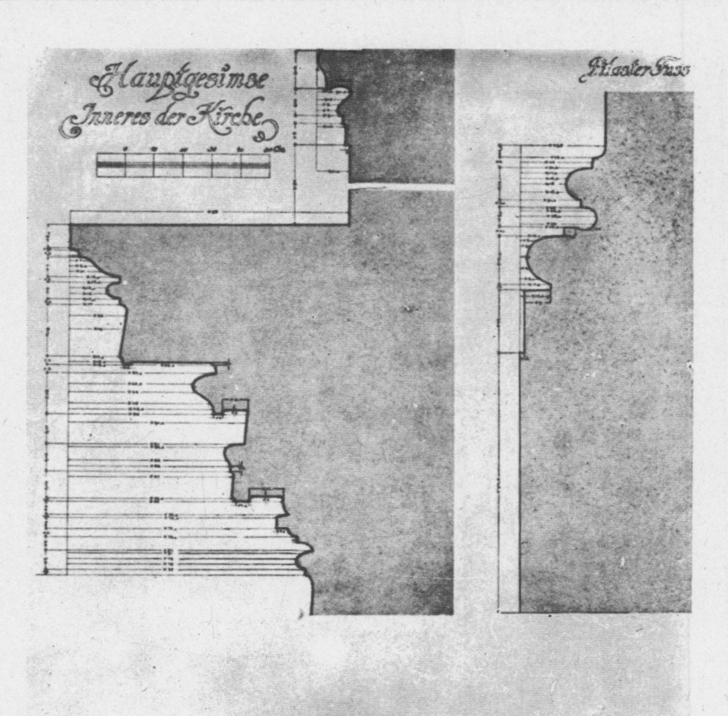

Left, scale representations in profile of Prandtauer's molded entablatures, bases, and plinths in the church, demonstrating the detail lavished on these architectural elements. Prandtauer's mastery of rich, mobile horizontal articulations has never been surpassed.

Below, one of Prandtauer's earliest plans for the church, published in 1702.

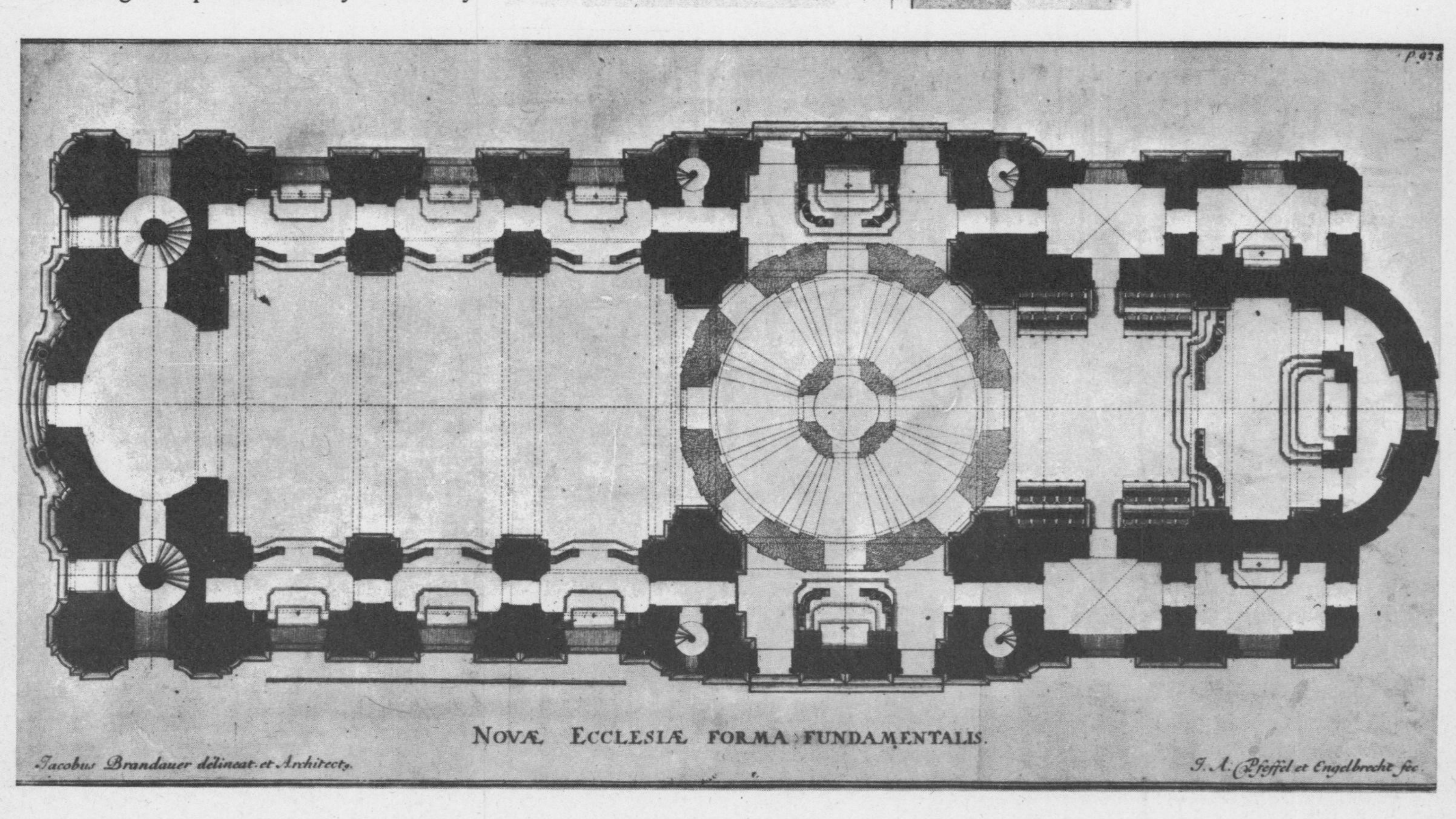

solved by rigging three trap doors that can be raised by bronze rings, allowing gusts of hot air to rise from furnaces burning in the rocky cellar below.

The curving balcony overlooks St. Coloman's Courtyard which is bounded by the façade of the church, the library and Marmorsaal, and the low structure which supports the balcony. The church's façade, although typically Baroque, is organized by three stories of superimposed pilasters and stringcourses (decorative bands of molding on the face of the building). Only the bulbous cupolas of the towers, the work of Munggenast, verge on the extravagant. The varied shapes of the side and central windows emphasize the organization of the façade into three vertical components, while the moldings accentuate the slight undulations of the wall surfaces.

The plan of Prandtauer's church is, like so many German Baroque churches, inspired by that of Il Gesù in Rome. Designed by Vignola in 1568, Il Gesù was a prototype for a Baroque hall church distinguished by the shortening of the transept arms and the transformation of the side aisles into shallow, interconnected chapels. Attention is thus focused on the main altar and—equally as important in the Counter-Reformation church at Melk—on the pulpit. Owing to the simplicity of the overall design, the Gesù plan allowed for ornate, even extravagant, theatrical effects.

The interior of the church at Melk, decorated under the direction of the theatrical designer Antonio Beduzzi, seems at first glance to be a riot of ornament. Above the entrance, the tremendous organ built by the Viennese organ maker, Gottfried Sonnholz, towers like some fantasy, bedecked with music-making angels and an orchestra of cherubs. At the other end of the nave, the gilt figures of saints and angels, executed by Peter Widerin after designs by Lorenzo Matielli, strike dramatic poses. Depicted above the high altar is the last farewell of Peter and Paul beneath a mighty gilt crown and the inscription *Non coronabitur nisi legitime certaverit* ("He shall not be crowned unless he shall have striven lawfully," Timothy 2:5).

Above, an 1843 miniature after a portrait of Abbot Wilhelm Eder, who was responsible for important repairs to the monastery during the mid-nineteenth century.

Right, a design for a side altar of the church, in a watercolor by Franz Mayer (1771).

Between the organ and the altar, hardly an inch of surface is left undecorated. The galleries above the side chapels are framed between elaborate openwork balustrades and other fantastic gilt ornaments designed by Beduzzi. In the shallow arms of the transept, the side altars of Saint Benedict and Saint Coloman are crowned by the rays of heavenly glorias. Johann Michael Rottmayr's ceiling frescoes, prepared from Beduzzi's designs, provide even more ornamentation. Yet the exuberant mass of decorative detail in the interior is saved from confusion by the underlying coherence of the church design.

The long vault over the nave actually consists of three smaller barrels arranged side by side. The focal point of the church is the crossing of nave and transept, where the frescoed dome is supported by pendentives. The pink and gray of the stucco walls and fluted pilasters form a dignified background to the profusion of gilt, while the white and pastels of the dome and vaults enhance the impression of height.

Prandtauer unified the great height of the church with the use of horizontal elements—moldings and an entablature—that frame the vaulted nave ceiling. The frieze of the entablature is decorated by ornamental gilt extensions of the capitals below, and together with the other strong horizontals, it links the pilastered walls with the high oval windows and the vaults of the nave.

The reconstruction of the monastery under Berthold Dietmayr was the high point in the later history of Melk. His successors fought a losing battle to maintain the prestige of their imposing monastery. Their sense of mission was not shared by Emperor Joseph II, who came to full

power in 1780. A man of his age, Joseph is remembered as one of the rational sovereigns of the eighteenth century who succeeded in curbing the power and wealth of the monastic orders.

The Napoleonic Wars brought Bonaparte—the first foreigner to capture the abbey—to Melk. Napoleon's soldiers earned a lasting place in local history for having consumed almost all the wine stored in the famous wine cellars beneath the buildings. The Napoleonic Wars also brought about the abolition of the Holy Roman Empire in 1806. As the Austrian state became gradually less dependent upon the church for support, the abbots of Melk lost much of their political influence. Their property and income were further curtailed by the anticlerical measures adopted in the wake of the 1848 revolutions. Fire—the old enemy of the isolated complex—aggravated Melk's financial problems, necessitating several partial rebuildings in the nineteenth and twentieth centuries. The most recent reconstruction took place in 1947.

Though the ancient community is a shadow of its former self, Jakob Prandtauer's monastery, built in a spirit of accountability to God and man, continues to express the faith of its founders and of those who live within its walls. A handful of men still quietly supervise parish work in the neighboring countryside, observe the Rule of St. Benedict, and maintain the 800-year-old school in the north wing of the complex. To those for whom Melk is a familiar landmark, the monastery is a reminder of a faith that has outlived war, fire, and changing political fortunes. Having weathered centuries of adversities and depredations, Melk is not simply an ancient monument inherited from the past, but a survivor.

Prandtauer's design for Melk captures the imagination largely because of the way in which it sets off the naturally dramatic quality of its setting. Not surprisingly, it became a favorite subject of eighteenth- and early nineteenth-century Austrian artists. Above left and below, two early treatments of the monastery dominating the hillside and town of Melk.

Cologne Cathedral

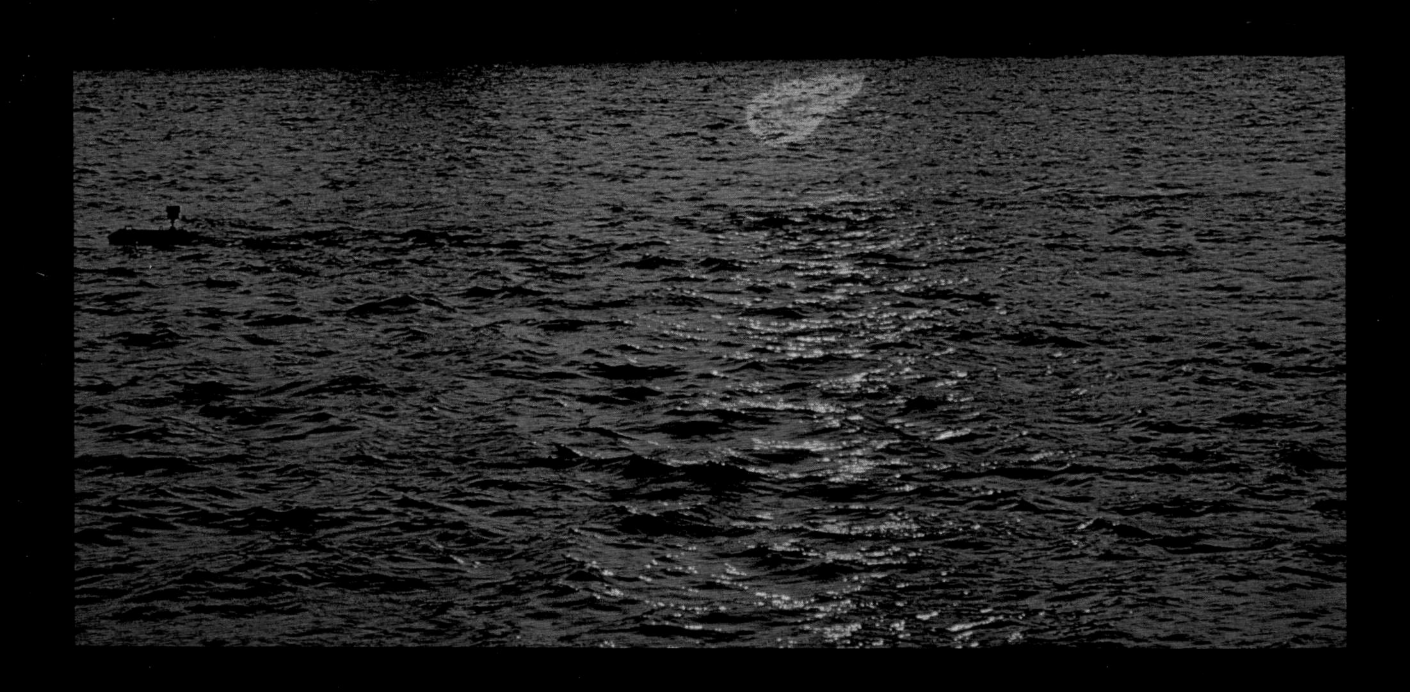

West Germany

The Cologne Cathedral is a natural landmark from any point in the city (preceding page). The cathedral was even more conspicuous during World War II, after artillery raids leveled the surrounding buildings in March 1945. Because the Allied forces were under express orders to spare the cathedral, it suffered no direct hits, though the roof and the windows were severely damaged. Many religious valuables, including thirteenth-century stained-glass windows, were transported to Hamburg for safekeeping. For centuries a symbol of the city and of German Catholicism, the rubble-filled cathedral was in use within days of the heavy bombing attacks.

The exposed buttress on the left of the western façade of Cologne Cathedral (right) is a result of war damage. Its counterpart on the right has been restored.

The original design for the cathedral called for five portals, but the outer two doors were replaced by tall windows. The rush of decorative detail is held in check by the underlying regularity of the design; the steep, pointed Gothic gables of each story pierce the story above, emphasizing the vertical. Above, the apse of the cathedral, seen from across the Rhine and (left) from a platform of the adjacent railroad station.

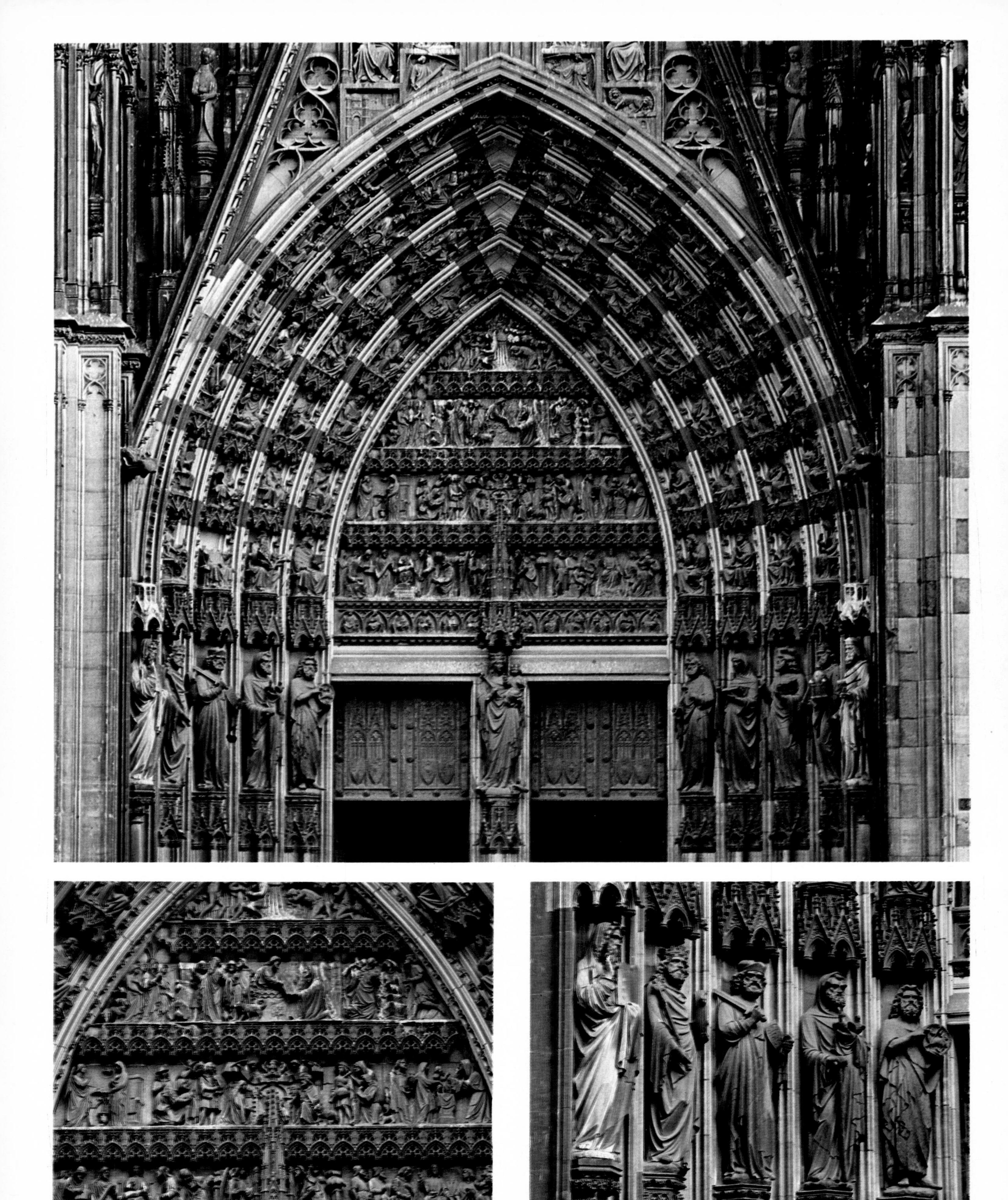

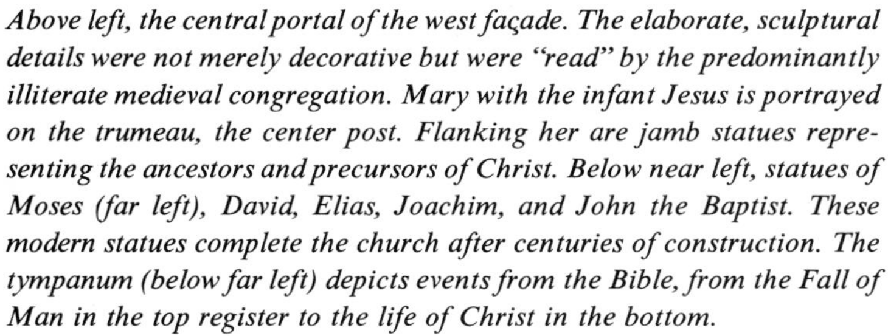

Above left, the central portal of the west façade. The elaborate, sculptural details were not merely decorative but were "read" by the predominantly illiterate medieval congregation. Mary with the infant Jesus is portrayed on the trumeau, the center post. Flanking her are jamb statues representing the ancestors and precursors of Christ. Below near left, statues of Moses (far left), David, Elias, Joachim, and John the Baptist. These modern statues complete the church after centuries of construction. The tympanum (below far left) depicts events from the Bible, from the Fall of Man in the top register to the life of Christ in the bottom.

The flying buttresses (top right), which seem mere fanciful decoration, transfer the lateral thrusts of the vaults, the heavy upper walls, and the roof downward. On the other hand, the impressive-looking spires (above, center and bottom right) are actually hollow. The quatrefoils and trefoils within circles that define the weblike open spaces of the spires are repeated in the flying buttresses and in the apex tracery of most of the tall windows.

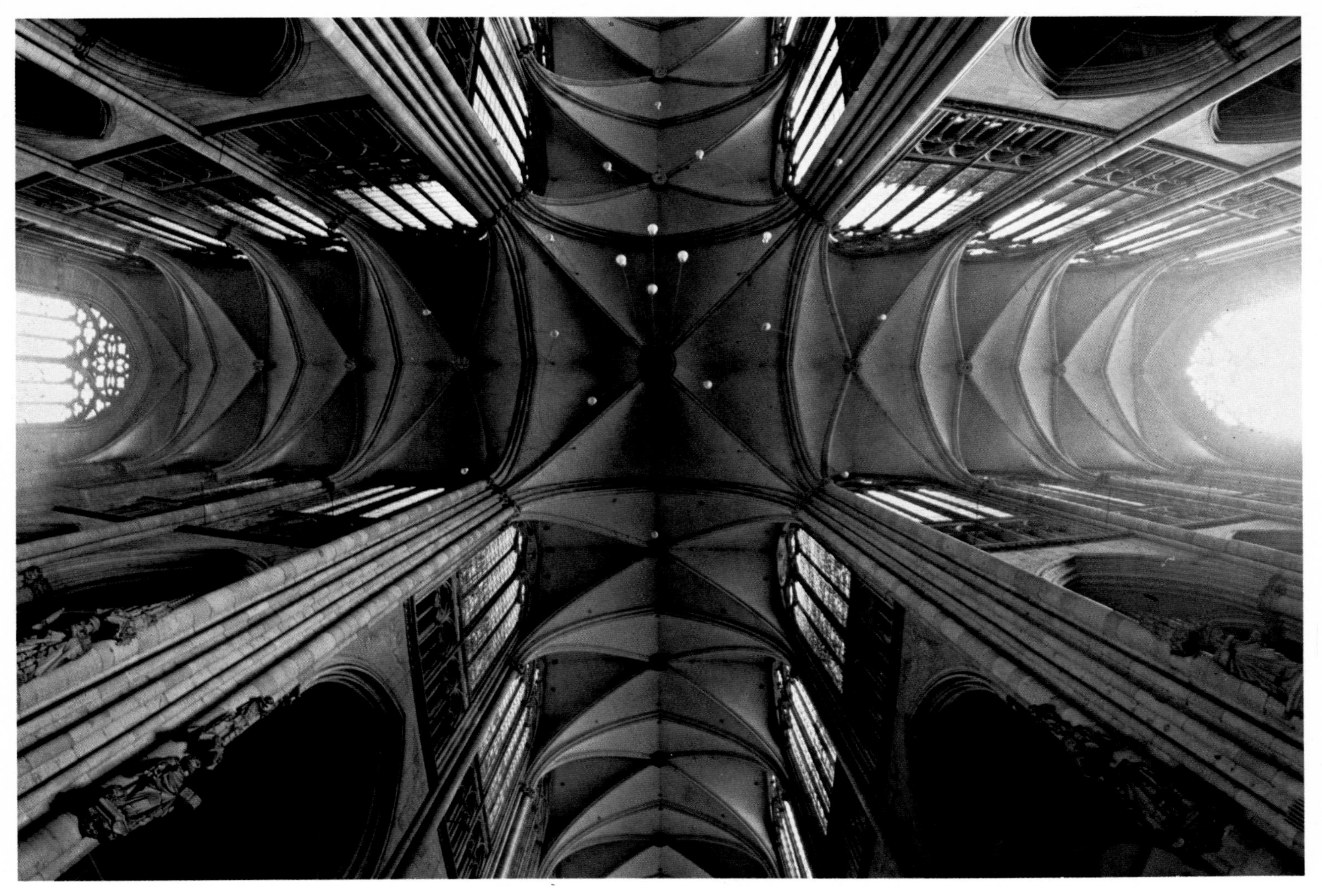

The interior of Cologne Cathedral (left) is a soaring vertical space unobstructed by balconies or supporting cross beams. (Much of the support is derived from the external buttresses.) Internal supporting piers are shaped into thin, clustered colonnettes which make them appear feather light. The principal piers rise unobstructed from the floor to modest capitals from which the vaults spring (below). The life-size figures of the Apostles, the Virgin, and Christ on the main piers are the work of German sculptors who trained in France and are among the last and finest examples of High Gothic sculpture. Above, the crossing—the juncture of the nave and the transept—where the beautiful ribbed vaulting is at its most impressive, looking like full-blown sails in the wind. The tall clerestory windows above the aisles add to the sense of weightlessness.

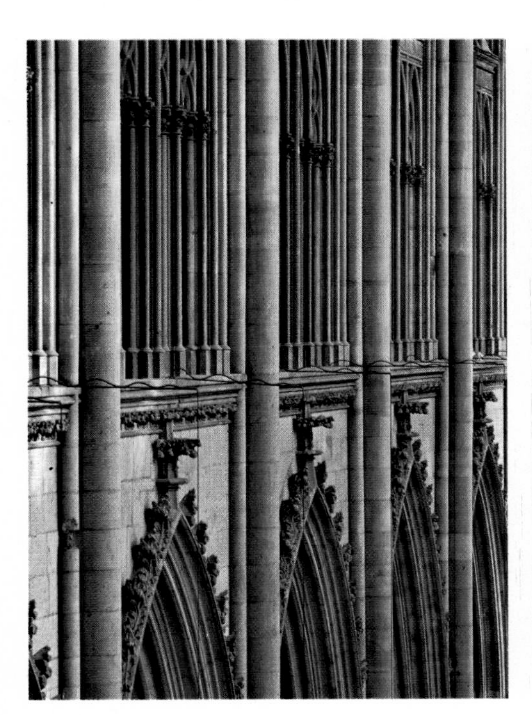

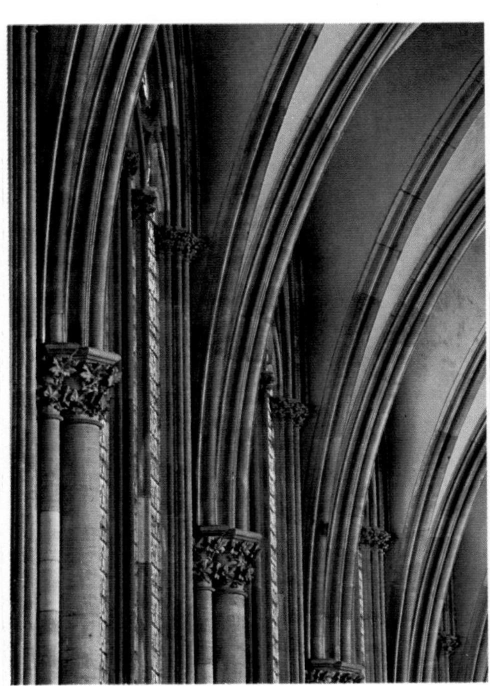

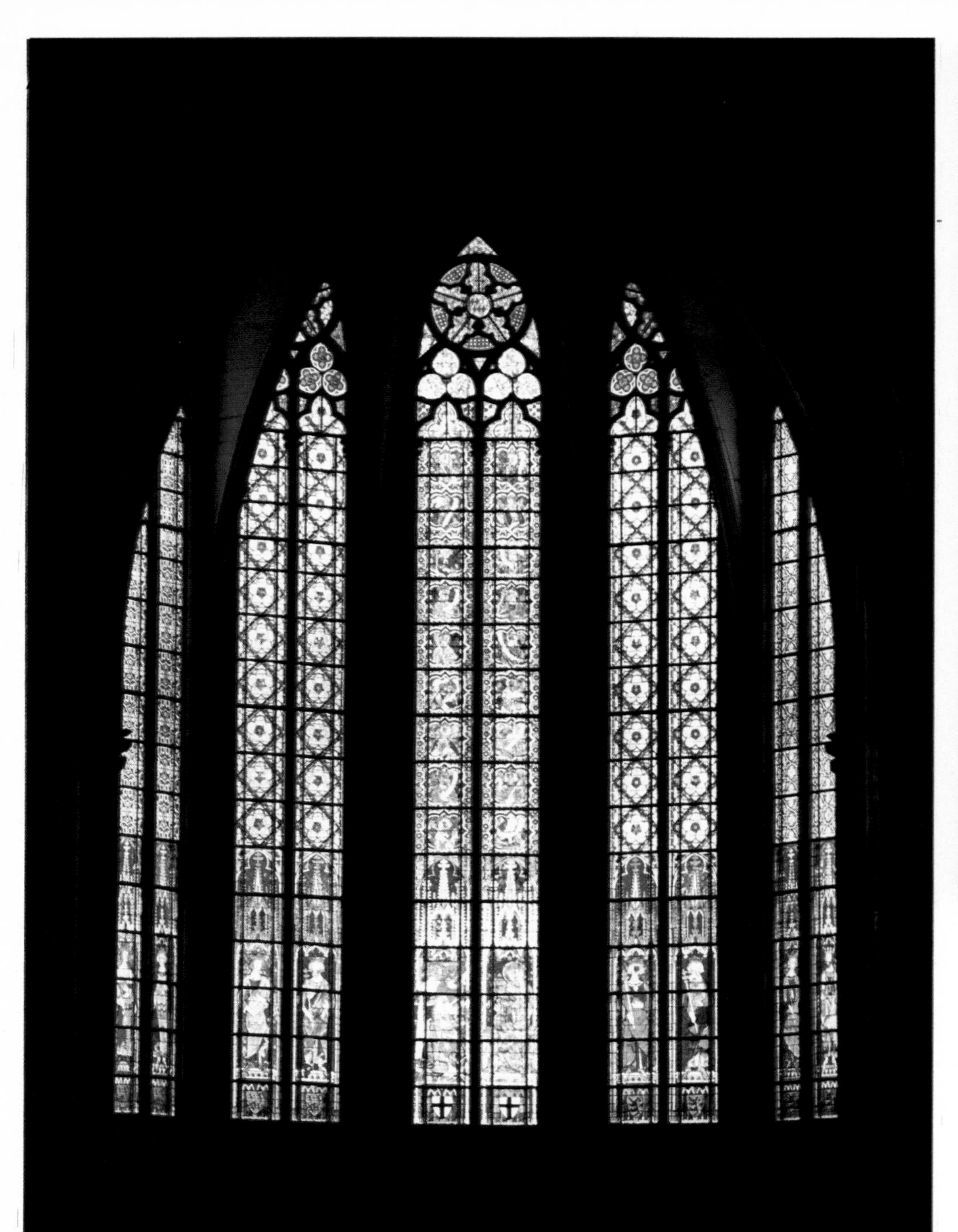

Cologne Cathedral has more than 100,000 square feet of stained-glass windows, added over many centuries. Despite the diverse styles of the glasswork, the repetition of the tall, pointed Gothic windows preserves an overall effect of regularity and unity.

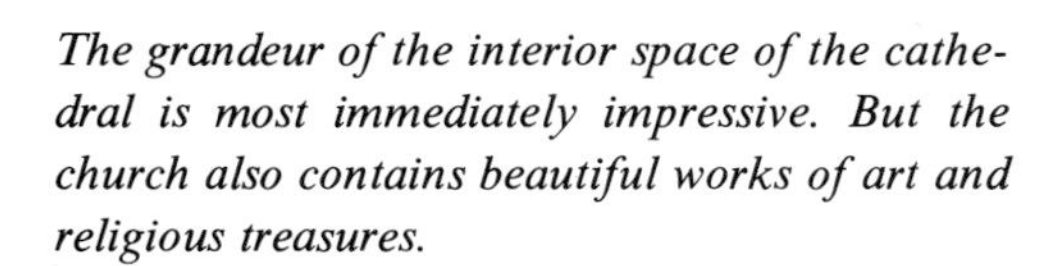

The grandeur of the interior space of the cathedral is most immediately impressive. But the church also contains beautiful works of art and religious treasures.

Top left and bottom right, the ark containing the relics of the Three Magi. This masterpiece of Gothic gold work dates from the early thirteenth century.

Immediately above, the Gerus Christ, so named because it was commissioned by Archbishop Gerus in the latter half of the tenth century.

Above right, the polychrome statue of Saint Philip that stands on one of the piers of the choir. Above the head of the saint, an angel plays a musical instrument. The statue is one of a series of sculptures in limestone which adorns the nave. They were commissioned by Master Arnold between 1270 and 1280.

Cologne Cathedral West Germany

When, in 1242, the master Gerhard drew up detailed plans of a new cathedral for the German city of Cologne, he must have realized that he would not live to see this, his finest project, completed. Great cathedrals were rarely built in one lifetime. Gerhard must also have thought that his plan would at some point be altered and that technical advances and new stylistic preferences would be introduced as construction progressed. But he could not have imagined that his cathedral would take 638 years to complete or that, when it was finally finished, it would be remarkably similar to his original plans.

Gerhard's design was modeled after Amiens Cathedral in northern France, on which he himself had probably worked. But Gerhard intended his cathedral to be far more impressive. It would be both longer and taller, measuring 448 feet in length and 515 feet to the top of the twin bell towers. And instead of three portals on the main façade, there would be five.

Inside, the lofty dimensions were to be accented by allowing the principal shafts of the piers to stretch unimpeded from the cathedral floor to the vault. These supports were made to appear even more delicate by sculpting them so that they looked like clusters of thin colonettes. The clerestory windows were to be taller and thinner than their French counterparts, again exaggerating the soaring height but also letting in more light. Throughout, the apexes of the Gothic arches, windows, and ceiling vaults were to be steeper and more sharply pointed. Here in Cologne, on the left bank of the Rhine, was to be built the finest example of High Gothic cathedral architecture in Germany.

Above, a woodcut from the Chronicles of Cologne *(1499) and an engraving (below) by Anton Wonsam (1531). Both show the still incomplete Cologne Cathedral rising above the medieval walls of the city. The church remained thus for the next three centuries.*

Top, the cathedral as it looked in 1800, unchanged since construction was halted in 1560. Immediately above, an 1855 engraving illustrating the progress made after construction was resumed in 1842.

Gerhard's cathedral was not the first but most probably the third to be built at Cologne. The city had been a bishopric since at least A.D. 313, when Bishop Maternus of Cologne was recorded as having attended a Roman synod, the only representative from a church in a northern country. In 785, Charlemagne elevated the seat to an archbishopric. This honor encouraged plans for a cathedral—the predecessor of Gerhard's church—on the same site, which then was the northern corner of the walled city.

From about the tenth century on, increasingly bitter conflicts flared up between Cologne's growing class of merchants and its archbishop. Cologne had become a prominent member of the Hanseatic League—the association of wealthy German mercantile cities—with the most varied trade of all the members. Cologne's merchant class was intent on securing commercial and political freedom; the archbishop was intent on retaining his temporal power. The archbishop's authority was augmented in the thirteenth century, when he became one of the seven electors of the Holy Roman Empire. It was not until 1288 that his power was curbed and Cologne acquired full self-government as an imperial city.

In this atmosphere of shifting political currents and expanding economic prosperity, the idea for a new and grander cathedral for Cologne took hold. At the beginning of the thirteenth century, the plan for the cathedral may have seemed an assertion of episcopal authority. But the merchants and bankers, with their growing civil power, probably approved of the idea as a symbol of their newly acquired influence. Their civic pride also made them eager to be especially generous toward the church in matters they felt were entirely within its realm.

In April 1248, a fire almost completely destroyed the vast, rambling Carolingian cathedral, confirming the resolution to build a new church. Fortunately, the cathedral's most treasured possession—the relics of the Three Magi, housed in a magnificent golden shrine—was saved. This jeweled and enameled reliquary was the work of Nicholas of Verdun, the most influential goldsmith of the Romanesque period. The relics themselves had been given to Cologne in 1164 by Holy Roman Emperor Frederick Barbarossa, who had seized them from Milan. They were said to have been first uncovered by the mother of the Emperor Constantine. Given the illustrious heritage of the relics, it seemed fitting that they be prominently displayed in the nave of the new cathedral.

Archbishop Konrad von Hochstaden laid the cornerstone for the new cathedral on August 15, 1248. The style chosen for the building—the Gothic—was new to Germany. It had seen its earliest development in France (ca. 1140) with the construction of the abbey church of St. Denis, just outside Paris. In the intervening century, builders had learned through trial and error how to increase the height of the ribbed vaults and pointed arches, and to narrow the thickness of the supporting walls, allowing more light to enter the interiors. They also developed a Gothic language in the detailing of cathedrals, especially in the window tracery and sculpture.

The construction of the immense cathedral—which would come to symbolize the

Left, the main façade of the cathedral as redrawn by Ernst Friedrich Zwiner from the medieval plans. In 1842, Frederick William IV of Prussia commissioned Zwiner to finish the cathedral. After Zwiner's death in 1861, Richard Voigtel supervised the completion of the project.

Above, a contemporary print of the solemn procession in Cologne on September 4, 1842, that marked resumption of work on the cathedral. Among those present were Archbishop Johann, Cardinal von Geisel, and King Frederick William IV.

religious, social, and economic power of Cologne—was destined to have a long and difficult history. Little was accomplished in the first twelve years of construction. In part, progress was slow because Gerhard was working at the same time on two other major projects: a cathedral at München-Gladbach and the Cistercian church at Altenburg. When Gerhard died on March 23, 1260, the apse was not even finished and would not be completed for more than sixty years.

Gerhard was succeeded by the master Arnold, who directed the cathedral works until 1299 and began the south wall and the southern bell tower. Arnold's son Johann was responsible for the only major change in Gerhard's original design: He eliminated the outer door of the southern bell tower, replacing it with a tall window. In the nineteenth century, when the northern bell tower was finally built, it was modeled on Johann's tower for the sake of symmetry—even though Gerhard's original plans had been preserved in Vienna.

By 1320, Johann had completed the choir, with its elaborately carved stalls and decorative frescoes. He also commissioned the life-size limestone statues of Jesus, Mary, and the Apostles, which are affixed to the main piers of the choir. These were executed by German artists trained in France.

From 1333 onward, progress was interrupted for nearly twenty years by a shortage of masons. Even after the renowned Michael Parler of Freiberg became master mason in 1353, it took ten years of painstaking work under his skillful direction just to decorate the portal of the southern bell tower. As in all Gothic cathedrals, each stone had to be completely finished and decorated before it was put in place.

By the mid-fifteenth century, the southern bell tower had reached somewhat more than a third of its intended height. Bells were installed, and a temporary wooden roof was added, which in fact was to remain for more than 400 years. A wooden crane, used to haul materials to the top of the tower, also remained in place—the tallest structure in Cologne for four centuries.

Less conspicuous work continued throughout the fifteenth century and into the sixteenth. The north wall and the northern bell tower were begun. A second so-called temporary roof sheltered the nave and aisles. Substantial decorative work was done on the apse, including the superb triptych adorning the Altar of the Patron Saints, which was executed by Stefan Lochner, the outstanding painter in the Cologne school of the early fifteenth century.

In 1560, work on the cathedral was suspended. The political and economic im-

Left, an early view of the completed cathedral from the south side.

Below, the ceremony held on October 15, 1880, marking the completion of the cathedral. The last stone to be placed in position was at the tip of the spire on the southern bell tower.

portance of the city was in decline. With the opening of trade routes in the New World, the economic balance of Europe was altered, and trade in central and northern Europe was severely damaged. The Reformation was profoundly changing customs and attitudes, and throughout the seventeenth century, long and bloody religious and dynastic wars ravaged Europe.

Despite the changing climate, Cologne remained faithful to Roman Catholicism. Indeed, in 1536, the city held an important council that discussed methods of checking the spread of Lutheranism. But the popularity of the Gothic waned in the face of the new artistic ideas introduced by the Renaissance.

The cathedral languished. Only essential repairs were made, including a much-needed, new wooden roof added in the mid-eighteenth century. Cologne Cathedral suffered several indignities. During the Napoleonic Wars, French troops used the cathedral as a stable. Then, in 1815, Cologne became part of the Kingdom of Prussia, then a predominantly Protestant nation.

Yet this low point for the cathedral coincided with a revival of interest in the Middle Ages. Gothic architecture, long neglected, was zealously studied, copied, and praised. In northern Germany, this revival of interest in the Gothic era was regarded as a high point in German culture, and preservation and restoration of Gothic monuments were considered to be national responsibilities.

The archbishopric of Cologne, which Napoleon had abolished, was reinstituted in 1821. Two years later, restoration work began on the cathedral, and in 1842, King Frederick William IV of Prussia promised to see to the long-awaited completion of the building. Ernst Friedrich Zwiner, the supervisory architect, painstakingly studied and copied Gerhard's original plans. Both Zwiner and Frederick William died in 1861, two years before the interior was completed. The king's brother and heir, William, encouraged continuation of the work under Richard Voigtel. On October 15, 1880, the cathedral was completed—638 years after construction had first begun.

The finished cathedral loomed above the other historic buildings in Cologne—a seemingly prime target for Allied bombing within this principal transportation depot of Germany. But Allied troops received specific orders to spare the cathedral. Through careful marksmanship, the Allies selectively leveled every building in the vicinity, but left the cathedral virtually intact. The relatively minor restorations were completed by August 15, 1948, in time for the seventh centenary of Archbishop von Hochstaden's laying of the cornerstone.

Today the cathedral faces a new danger. Industrial pollution is damaging the stonework and stained glass, necessitating almost continuous restorative care. But the citizens of Cologne accept the challenge philosophically. "When the cathedral is finished," they say, "the world will end."

Hagia Sophia

Istanbul

Often called the "eye of faith," Hagia Sophia (preceding page) was for centuries the most important church of the Byzantine Empire. With the founding of the modern Turkish state under Kemal Attaturk, the sixth-century basilica, whose name means "holy wisdom," was transformed into a museum.

The interlocking arrangement of domes in Hagia Sophia (left) provides an eloquent display of the basic principles of Byzantine architecture. After the fall of Constantinople to the Ottoman Turks in 1453, Hagia Sophia served as a mosque. The four tall minarets (above) were added during this period.

East meets West under Hagia Sophia's celebrated dome (right). At Hagia Sophia, the combination of the Eastern centralized church plan and Western elongated plan produced the only true domed basilica in Christian architecture. The melding of cultural influences was the glory of Byzantine art, but in later centuries the church's position at the crossroads of Europe and the Middle East had calamitous consequences. Soldiers of the Fourth Crusade vandalized the sanctuary in 1204, and the Moslems whitewashed the basilica's mosaics, which they considered idolatrous.

Sixth-century chroniclers liked to describe the ethereal effect produced by sunlight streaming through Hagia Sophia's high windows and reflecting off the gold, silver, and gemstone decorations beneath. Most of these opulent treasures are now gone, but the illusion of weightlessness and the flood of light in the nave are still dramatic. The mass of the dome is seemingly denied by the ring of windows in its base, which in turn seems to balance tenuously on four elegant pendentives (above right).

حسين
علي
رضي الله تعالى عنه
عمر
الفاروق

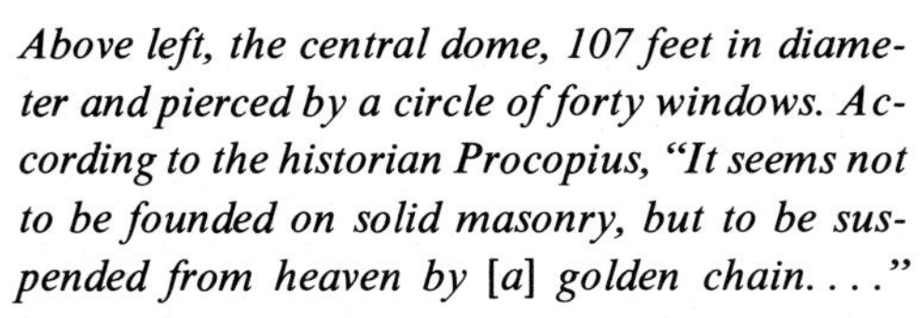

Above left, the central dome, 107 feet in diameter and pierced by a circle of forty windows. According to the historian Procopius, "It seems not to be founded on solid masonry, but to be suspended from heaven by [a] golden chain. . . ."

Below left and this page, details of Hagia Sophia's 104 monolithic marble columns. Some of these supports, particularly those in the lower arcades (above right), are reinforced by bronze rings to prevent the columns from splitting because of the tremendous weight above. Though the capitals incorporate standard Classical elements, the acanthus-leaf motif is transformed by a new use of drills; at Hagia Sophia, the acanthus has a wind-blown, filigreelike form which contributes to the overall feeling of weightlessness in the church. The capitals in the lower arcades (immediately above) include Justinian's monogram.

Hagia Sophia's once-dazzling mosaics, now in disrepair (left), inspired both Moslem and Christian imitations, including those at the basilica of San Marco in Venice. Among the oldest mosaic images recently uncovered and restored are the ninth-century seated Virgin and Child (top left) and the brooding, comparatively naturalistic thirteenth-century Christ of the Deësis panel (top right). Immediately above, an emperor, believed to be Leo II (886–912), prostrating himself before Christ. Right, a ninth-century mosaic of Saint Ignatius Theophorus of Antioch, one of fourteen bishops portrayed on the mural curtain walls of the nave.

Hagia Sophia Istanbul

On December 26, 537, the Emperor Justinian marched in a grand ceremonial procession from Constantinople's old basilica of St. Anastasius to the Church of the Holy Wisdom. This new cathedral, built under Justinian's direction, was about to be consecrated as a Great Church of Eastern Orthodoxy and the centerpiece of a revitalized Constantinople. When the finished church, with its apparently weightless dome, came into view, Justinian is said to have paused and exclaimed, "Solomon, I have surpassed thee." The boast was not empty vanity. Hagia Sophia, as it is known in Greek, was destined to be the premier church of the Byzantine world for centuries.

In many respects, Justinian's career as temple builder, lawgiver, and emperor paralleled that of Solomon. During the later years of his reign, Justinian was even called in to mediate a dispute that resembled the famous case in which Solomon was asked to choose between two mothers who claimed the same baby. This time, the body in contention was that of Christ Himself. Justinian was pressured by the Roman Pope Vigilius, on the one hand, to support the Latin belief in the dual nature of Christ and by the Monophysites, on the other hand, to accept the Savior's wholly divine nature. Unfortunately, Justinian was no Solomon. Though a brilliant administrator, the emperor tended to be crippled by indecision during crises. And in fact, his vacillations in the face of the Monophysite controversy eventually led to the deterioration of his relations with the West and the disaffection of Middle Eastern Monophysites.

None of these problems were evident the day Hagia Sophia was consecrated in 537. On the contrary, the ceremony marked the consolidation of Justinian's autocratic powers. The new cathedral replaced another church of the same name, which had been founded by Constantine in 324. This hallowed monument was destroyed in 532 during the Nika Rebellion, an uprising inspired by Justinian's spendthrift and authoritarian ways. During the Nika riots, Justinian was characteristically irresolute. At one point, he was actually ready to flee for his life, but his empress, Theodora, who had risen from lowly origins as a circus dancer and courtesan, had no intention of giving up all she had gained. With a fiery speech, the empress rallied the imperial generals and ended the revolt with the massacre of 30,000 rebels.

Far from chastened by this experience, Justinian immediately commissioned a new and expensive church, "such as has never been seen since Adam and will never be seen again." As architects, Justinian hired the mathematician Anthemius of Tralles and a physicist named Isidorus of Miletus. They satisfied their commission by constructing a church that blended both Eastern and Western architectural traditions. From the East they adopted a domed centralized plan. They capped the vast interior space with a dome 107 feet in diameter but dramatically flattened to a mere fifty feet in height. From the West, they borrowed an elongated processional space. Thus Hagia Sophia became the first true domed basilica in the world.

Pierced at its base by a circle of forty windows, the unusual dome appears to be suspended in midair. It actually rests on pendentives that rise out of four massive

The Emperor Justinian (above) commissioned Hagia Sophia, Church of the Holy Wisdom, in 532 to replace a church of the same name, founded by Constantine in Constantinople more than 200 years before. Right, a sixteenth-century Italian monk's depiction of Galata, a port across the Golden Horn from Constantinople that was frequented by Genoese and Venetian seamen.

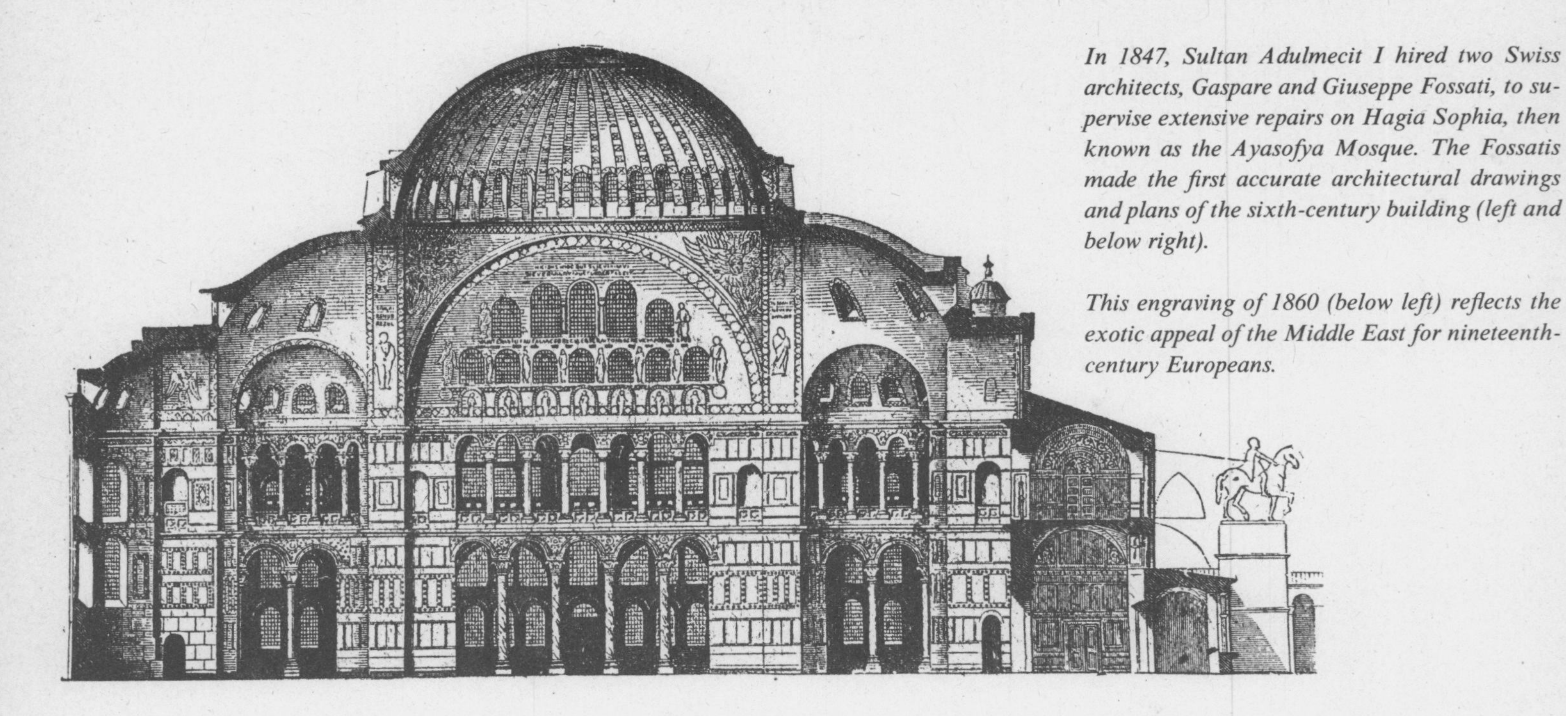

In 1847, Sultan Adulmecit I hired two Swiss architects, Gaspare and Giuseppe Fossati, to supervise extensive repairs on Hagia Sophia, then known as the Ayasofya Mosque. The Fossatis made the first accurate architectural drawings and plans of the sixth-century building (left and below right).

This engraving of 1860 (below left) reflects the exotic appeal of the Middle East for nineteenth-century Europeans.

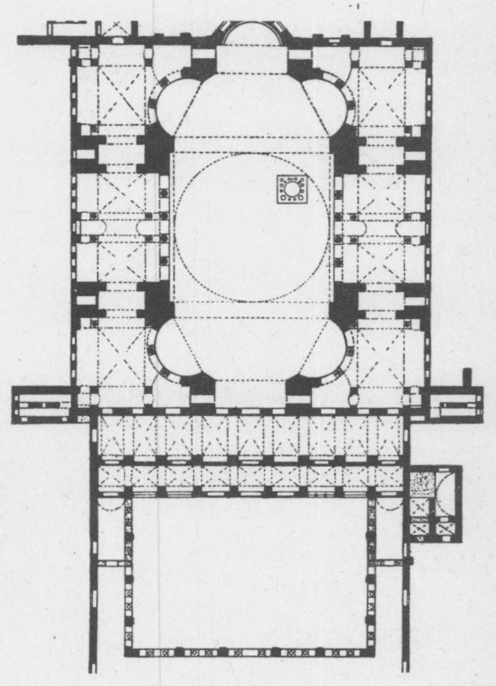

piers strengthened by joints of molten lead. In effect, the basilica is a hollow cube of space crowned by an equally hollow half-sphere. The north and south sides of this cube have curtain walls broken by windows and double-storied arcades. On the second story are segregated galleries for men and women. The east and west sides of the cube open into half-domes and again into smaller, rounded extensions. The result is a subtle rectangular interior, 250 by 230 feet.

The 104 monolithic columns in the nave were of marble and porphyry, as were the floors and walls. The completed bema, or sanctuary, glittered with 40,000 pounds of silver, and the main altar was made of gold, inlaid with precious gems. Most astonishingly, the construction of Hagia Sophia took only five years, as it was organized with such precision that as many as 10,000 laborers were employed at one time on the project.

Hagia Sophia's dome has always been its most admired feature. Writing soon after the consecration ceremony, the historian Procopius reserved his highest praise for this dome, noting that "it seems not to be founded on solid masonry, but to be suspended from heaven by [a] golden chain. . . ."

Twenty-one years after the consecration, the great dome partially collapsed during an earthquake. Isidorus of Miletus, brought back to repair the damage, strengthened the dome and raised it another twenty feet, modifying its flat appearance. From this time on, the restored dome, though still breathtakingly beautiful, inspired awe mixed with fear. Over the centuries, this apprehension has proved entirely justified. The western half-dome failed in 886, to be restored eight years later. After another earthquake undermined the main dome during the fourteenth century, heavy buttresses were added to the exterior of the church. None of these difficulties, however, can obscure Hagia Sophia's reputation as one of the greatest architectural achievements of all time. The church has, after all, survived for over 1,400 years.

As a good son of the Eastern Orthodox Church, Procopius naturally gave the lion's share of credit for Hagia Sophia to divine inspiration. In truth, the architects of the church were heavily influenced by secular and pagan models, including old Roman basilicas and the Roman Pantheon. Upon completion, Hagia Sophia often seemed to celebrate the wisdom of the Emperor Justinian and his successors over and above the wisdom of God. The very existence of the church, which was paid for by ruthless taxation and expropriation of land, reminded everyone from peasant to noble of the absolute nature of imperial power. This message was incorporated into the iconography of the nave's mosaics, for example, which pictured emperors and empresses as often as saints and holy men.

While a considerable portion of the sixth-century mosaics still survives, all figural compositions at Hagia Sophia date from the ninth century. These later works continued to stress the continuity between divine and secular authority. A lunette over the southern portal of the nave sets the theme, showing the Virgin and Child flanked by Constantine, who holds a model of Constantinople, and by Justinian, who presents the Virgin with a miniature of Hagia Sophia. Throughout the cathedral, the dominant image of Christ was not the suffering Savior or even the judge of souls at the Second Coming, but Christ the Pantocrator, ruler of the universe. The greatest amount of purely religious symbolism found in Hagia Sophia is expressed in its architecture. Its great dome is the bosom of heaven, and the Holy Trinity is honored repeatedly in the church's three stories as well as in its triple bays, portals, and windows.

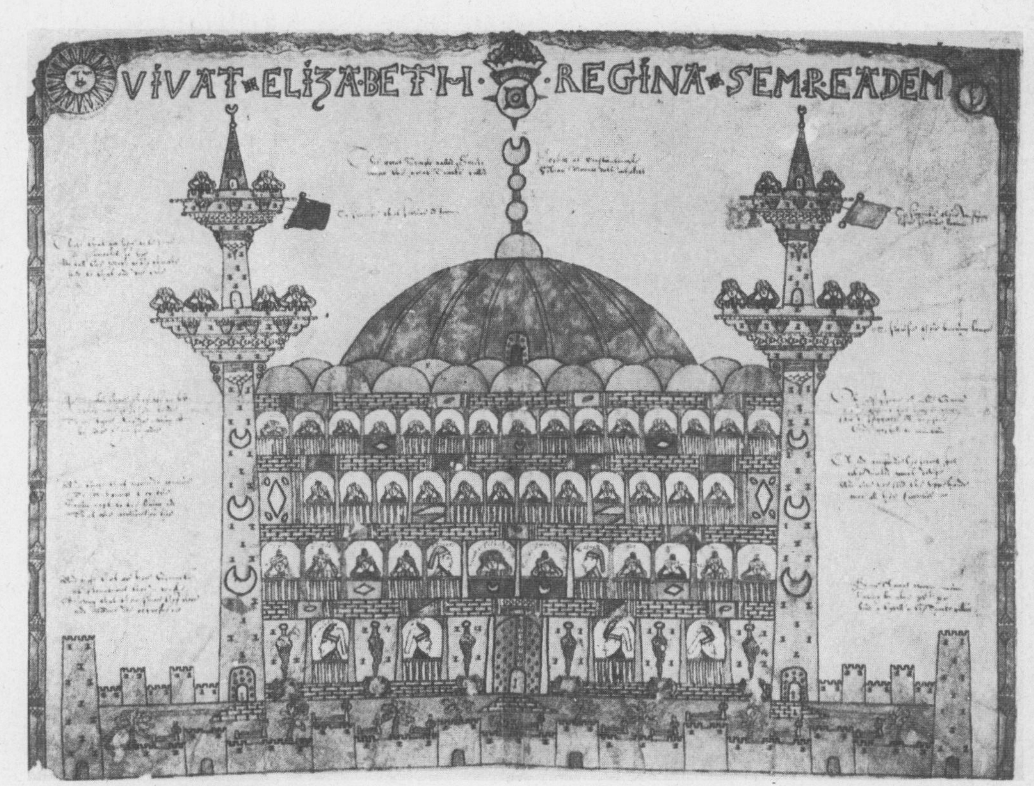

A history of Constantinople, written by an English prisoner in Elizabethan times, included this fanciful illustration of Hagia Sophia (above) and regaled British readers with the exploits of two powerful Ottoman rulers. These included Mohammed II, the Conqueror (left), and Suleiman the Magnificent (below). Below left, the angel Gabriel, a familiar figure in Moslem as well as Christian iconography.

The conversion of Hagia Sophia into a mosque included the construction of fountains (left), where worshipers ritually cleansed themselves before entering the sanctuary.

Under Ottoman rule, Constantinople's name was changed to Istanbul, meaning "in the city." The nineteenth-century view below shows Turkish and European vessels entering the Golden Horn.

By the end of the decline of the Byzantine Empire in the mid-fifteenth century, Hagia Sophia was reduced to a shadow of its former grandeur. Epitomizing the change was the replacement in the seventeenth century of the prominent mosaic Pantocrator, which once covered the apex of the dome, with a Koranic inscription. Five centuries after the Iconoclastic Movement, Constantinople once again fell prey to a campaign of destruction waged in the name of religion. The army of the Fourth Crusade (1202–1204), instigated by the one-time Byzantine colony of Venice, sacked the city. Not even the churches were spared. Troops quartered their horses under the dome of Hagia Sophia, and the nave was stripped of its precious gold and silver treasures. The Crusaders were careful to save such venerable objects as a large fragment of the true cross, the basket that had held Christ's miraculous loaves and fishes, and the veil of the Virgin. Much more, however, was wantonly destroyed. It is said that the soldiers installed a prostitute on the throne of the Patriarch to preside over their drunken orgy of book burning and vandalism.

Constantinople never really recovered from this raid, and its fall to the Ottoman Turks two and a half centuries later was almost anticlimactic. The last Christian service to be held in Hagia Sophia was on May 28, 1453, and the next day a Turkish army of 80,000 men defeated a Byzantine force of fewer than 7,000. Upon entering the city four days later, the Sultan Mohammed II went directly to the Church of the Holy Wisdom to thank his god, Allah, for the victory. Within the year the church was formally reconsecrated as the Ayasofya Mosque. The Moslems erected four tall minarets at the corners of the church, covered the marble floors with carpets, and hung a great medallion bearing Arabic inscriptions from each of the four great piers of the nave. Unlike the Crusaders, these conquerors never engaged in senseless destruction or persecution. But since the mosaics of Hagia Sophia violated the Moslem taboo against pictorial representation, they were promptly whitewashed, and some images are still concealed after six centuries.

In 1935, Hagia Sophia was deconsecrated and became a museum under the control of the Turkish government. Today, the golden sunshine that streams through the windows of the great dome falls on visitors of all religions and nationalities. Whether or not they are believers, nearly all who come to Hagia Sophia experience something akin to the mystical awe which inspired the sixth-century poet, Paul the Silentiary: "Through the spaces of the great church, come rays of light, expelling clouds of care and filling the mind with joy."

Cuzco Cathedral

Peru

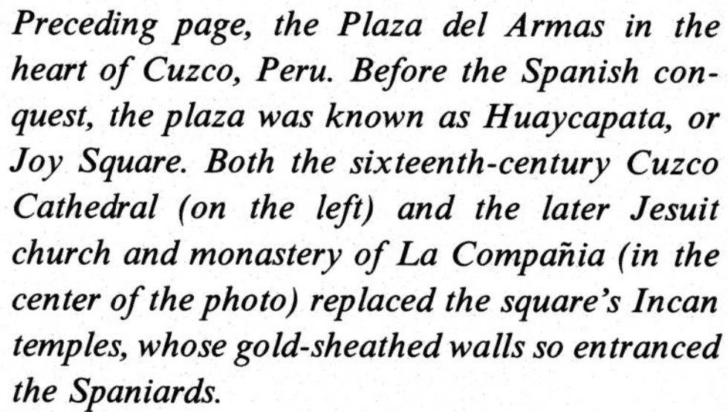

Preceding page, the Plaza del Armas in the heart of Cuzco, Peru. Before the Spanish conquest, the plaza was known as Huaycapata, or Joy Square. Both the sixteenth-century Cuzco Cathedral (on the left) and the later Jesuit church and monastery of La Compañia (in the center of the photo) replaced the square's Incan temples, whose gold-sheathed walls so entranced the Spaniards.

Francisco Pizarro, who entered the city in 1533, is said to have ordered the building of Cuzco Cathedral on the site of the destroyed Temple of Viracocha, the Incan creator-god. The cathedral's Baroque façade (above) was not completed until a century later.

Bottom right, typical carved wood statues of the Holy Family from the attached early eighteenth-century Church of the Triumph. The cathedral's elaborate towers (top right) were purposely built low as a protection against earthquakes, common in this region.

The pinnacles on the roof of Cuzco Cathedral (above left) and the diminutive figures of priests over the main portal (above right) are rare touches of delicacy on the exterior of the church. Dark red, Andean building stone gives both the cathedral and the somewhat newer Church of the Triumph (left) a somber appearance.

An Indian porter skillfully ascends the cathedral steps (near right), which are steep and narrow in the manner favored by pre-Columbian builders. Far right, other Quechua-speaking Indians, descendants of the Incas and their vassals, enjoying a few minutes of respite in the shadow of the cathedral. One of the street musicians (bottom far right) is playing the quena, *an Incan-style flute. His companion's instrument is a makeshift combination of old and new.*

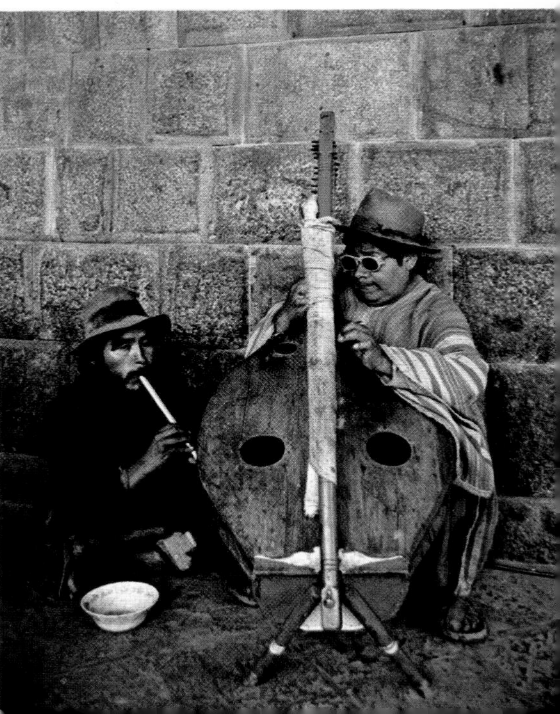

Inside the cathedral, the feeling of spaciousness is created by the high vaulted ceiling whose decorative pattern (above left and immediately below) survives from the Gothic technique of rib-vaulting. Gilded screens inside the main door of the cathedral (below left) enclose the choir. The placement of the choir, which conceals the main altar from the view of worshipers entering the church, is typically Spanish.

The central vault of the Church of the Triumph (above right) rests on squinches decorated with paintings by Cuzco artists. Many more works from the School of Cuzco, a group composed largely of Christianized Incan painters, are displayed in the chapels and side aisles of the cathedral (below right).

Incan artists and craftsmen often interpreted Christian symbolism in light of their own cultural expectations. The figures of the Virgin (top left) and Christ (top right), for example, are arrayed in rich robes. These two angels (above center) are a study in contrasting media: The sculpture on the left is an expressive, realistic depiction while the painting on the right is a stylized, rather naive portrait framed by ornate gilt. Left, a section of the Baroque cedar-wood altar that is the cathedral's most notable Rococo art treasure.

Although the cathedral is dedicated to the Assumption of the Virgin, the suffering Christ has always been the image inspiring the sympathy and devotion of the converted Incas. Two popular objects of pilgrimage are the Lord of the Earthquakes *(above), said to protect Cuzco from the quakes that periodically ravage Peru, and the* Black Christ *(top right), realistically adorned with a wig of human hair.*

Following page, the illuminated façade of the Jesuit Church of La Compañia on the Plaza del Armas. This late seventeenth-century structure, more ornate if not more imposing than the Cuzco Cathedral, testifies to the pervasive influence of the Society of Jesus in colonial Peru.

Cuzco Cathedral
Peru

High in the Andes of southern Peru, in the Urubamba Valley, there is a city known in the Quechua language as Cuzco, the Navel of the World. Cuzco was the capital of an Incan empire that, at its height in the early sixteenth century, stretched from Ecuador to the northern regions of present-day Chile and Argentina.

The realm of the Incas was prosperous, cultured, and so intensively organized that it has been called "the most complete welfare state mankind has known." Every subject of the Lord Inca, down to the lowliest peasant in the most remote village, was guaranteed complete economic security. In return, one-third of all wealth produced in the kingdom officially belonged to the Inca. And from this imperial share, the best of everything—farm produce, cloth, artworks—made its way to Cuzco. There was even a system for recruiting the most beautiful young girls from all over the kingdom to become Chosen Women. After receiving an elitist education, the most promising achieved the honored status of Virgins of the Sun, serving and maintaining Cuzco's many temples.

Cuzco was a dazzling city. When the conquering soldiers of Francisco Pizarro entered the Incas' capital in 1533, they were astounded at the sight of their prize. In a letter to Madrid, the official scribe of the Spaniards' expedition reported tersely that Cuzco "is large enough and handsome enough to compare with any Spanish city." But by the time this letter reached its destination, the city's treasured monuments had already been destroyed. In their greed, the Spaniards had stripped the gold-plated walls of Cuzco's temples and palaces.

As a ransom for the Incan ruler Atahualpa, the conquistadors appropriated the gold, raided homes and religious sanctuaries, and, within a matter of weeks, reduced the art treasures of an entire civilization to a pile of ingots. Despite the gold ransom and his friendship with some of the most influential Spanish cavaliers, including Hernando de Soto and Francisco's elder brother Hernando Pizarro, the captive Atahualpa could not be saved. On August 23, 1533, Francisco Pizarro had him executed.

For all its magnificence, the Incan empire was relatively young. When Cuzco was founded in about A.D. 1100, the Incas were just one of several competing Andean civilizations. Neither the Incas nor their neighbors ever developed a written language. Thus, our knowledge of how and why this one tribe came to dominate all the rest is derived largely from those legends that survived the Spanish conquest. Many of these stories were recorded by Garcilaso de la Vega, the son of an Incan princess and a Spanish soldier of noble family who were married shortly after Pizarro's entry into Cuzco.

According to Garcilaso, the Incan capital had been the Sun God's gift to man-

Left, the golden city of Cuzco as it appeared to the first conquistadors to enter the Incan capital in 1533. Only the vanguard of the Spanish force ever saw Cuzco with its treasures intact. Within a matter of weeks, this advance party had stripped the temples and palaces of their golden friezes. Above, an Incan bird dance as it would have been performed at the time of the Spanish conquest.

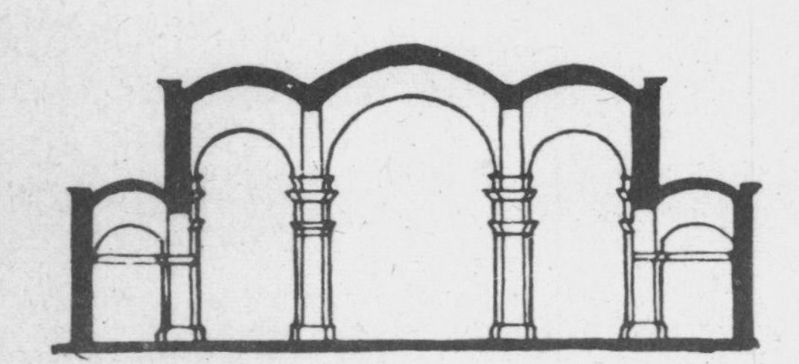

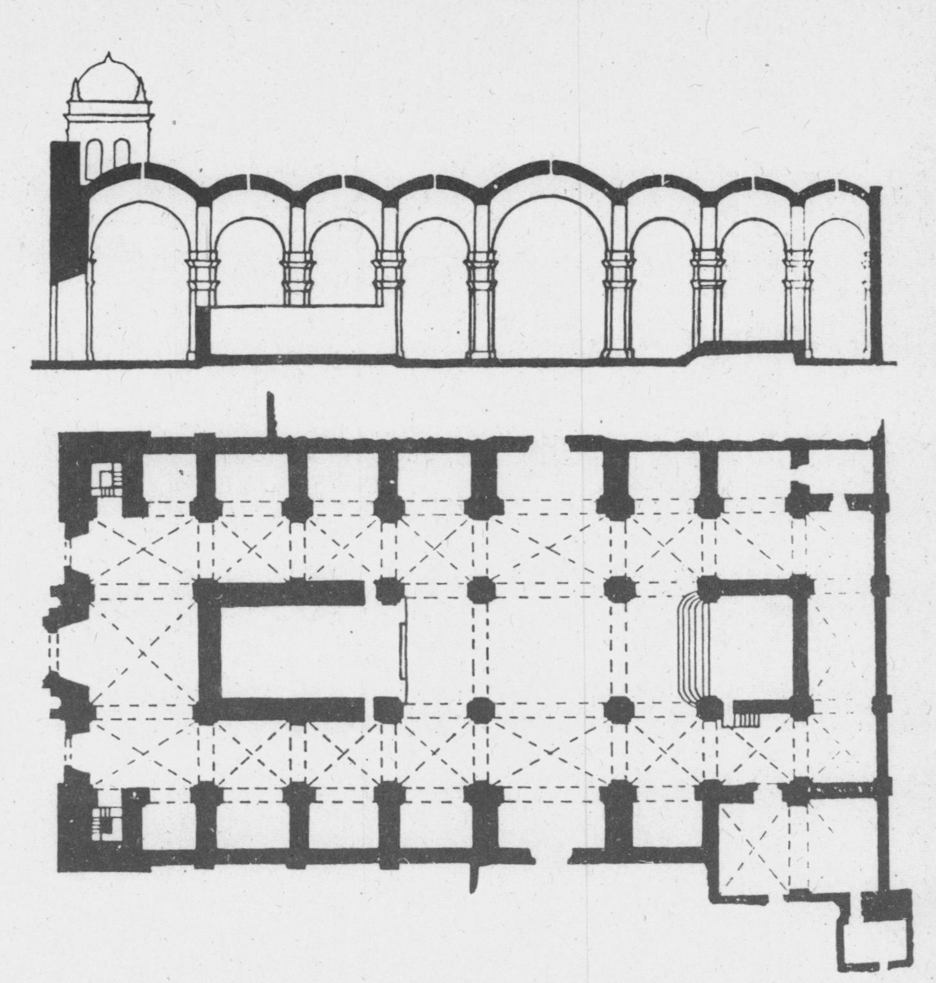

Below right, a plan of Cuzco Cathedral. The design of the cathedral, as finally built, is usually attributed to Francisco Becerra, one of many architects involved in the century-long building project. Above, a lateral section and above right, a longitudinal section. The large open-ended rectangle of the choir, just inside the main entrance, faces the slightly elevated sanctuary.

kind. One day, seeing that human beings lived in squalor with nothing but bark and leaves to cover their nakedness, this all-powerful god had sent his own son and daughter, Manco Capac and Mama Ocla, down to Lake Titicaca. Here, they were instructed to teach the civilized arts of agriculture, weaving, pottery, and metalwork. As the couple traveled northward, Manco Capac carried a golden staff, and when he found a place with soil so deep that he could bury the length of the staff in the earth, he founded a new city. This place was called *cosco,* or navel. As Garcilaso explained, it was well named because "Peru is long and narrow like a human body and Cuzco is situated in the middle of its belly."

By the time Garcilaso was a boy, the Incas had already embraced Christianity. Since they had grown accustomed to the practice of conquerors forcing their gods on vanquished tribes, the Incas were not surprised when the Spaniards made a similar demand. Spanish priests were delighted when the Indians quickly submitted to baptism, and for the most part they chose to overlook the Incas' incomplete understanding of their adopted religion. As it happened, many of the Indians saw little difference between the Christian God (the Giver of Light) and their own Father Sun. Indeed, when Indian artisans set out to create images of the Virgin Mary, they often pictured her as looking much like a Virgin of the Sun, wearing a jeweled headband and shawl and holding a distaff, the Incan symbol of womanly virtue.

At 11,000 feet above sea level, Cuzco was too inaccessible to serve as the capital of the conquistadors. Even while active resistance continued in the mountains of the Urubamba Valley, Francisco Pizarro was building Lima to serve as his administrative and military base. But Cuzco, with its mosquito-free climate, solid stone buildings, and neatly laid out streets and plazas, was too desirable to abandon. Not being able to improve on what was already there, the Spaniards either threw up adobe buildings over the magnificent Incan stone foundations or plundered the old walls, which had been erected entirely without mortar, to build their less magnificent structures.

Only in the broad public square at the heart of Cuzco did Spanish pride assert itself. The Incas had called this plaza Huaycapata, or Joy Square, but the Spanish soon changed the name to the Plaza del Armas. They also proceeded to raze the pagan temples and palaces that ringed the square and replace them with Christian monuments meant to impress the Incas with the glories of European culture. One of the first such structures was to be a cathedral erected on the site of the old temple of the creator-god Tici Viracocha.

In 1553, the pope granted permission for the establishment of a cathedral in Cuzco. But the local authorities, demoralized by squabbles and civil unrest, made little progress. They did not get around to laying the cornerstone of the cathedral until 1560. And eleven years later when the viceroy, Francisco de Toledo, came to inspect the work, he found that not much more had been accomplished. Dismayed, Toledo ordered that the cathedral be completed within six years.

Following this edict, Cuzco clerics regularly sent news of their progress to Lima and Madrid. Based on these optimistic reports, a new bishop, Alonzo Ocon, journeyed to Peru in 1644 expecting to celebrate mass in a finished cathedral. Ocon

The horrors perpetrated throughout South America by the Spanish conquerors were exposed by the Dominican Bishop Bartolomé de Las Casas, as shown in his History of the Indies *(right).*

found the walls less than half-built and, once again, a scandal ensued. Aware of the futility of issuing edicts, Ocon himself took action, levying heavy taxes on the Spanish aristocracy in Peru and pressing Indian laborers into service. By 1654, the cathedral was finally ready for use.

Considering the long history of its construction, Cuzco Cathedral might have been an aesthetic disaster. At least four architects had worked on the project, each forced to adapt his work not only to the ideas of his predecessors but also to the restrictions of building a European-style church with Indian masons and Peruvian building materials. As documentation of the project is sketchy when not overtly falsified, few details of the cathedral's construction are known. Most experts, however, attribute its basic plan—a rectangle with a nave and two side aisles—to Francisco Becerra, an architect who was commissioned as late as 1582. This plan, which is quite similar to Becerra's design for the cathedral at Lima, is typically Spanish, although it is a departure from the cross-shaped churches so common throughout the rest of Europe.

It is said that Spanish architects favored a less linear, rectangular form because of

Below left, a woodcut depicting the rival followers of Pizarro and Diego de Almagro, between whom a civil war broke out soon after the conquest. Below, an Inca, dumbfounded by Spanish greed: "Do you eat gold?" he asks. "Yes," the conquistador replies.

Above, a Corpus Christi Day procession through the streets of Cuzco. Catholicism, as practiced by seventeenth-century Indian converts, was infused with pagan rituals and beliefs as evidenced here by the ceremonial headdress and bare feet.

their knowledge of Moorish mosques, such as the Cathedral of Cordova in Spain. The fact that such churches, which began as mosques, did not emphasize height proved to have the additional virtue in Peru of making them more resistant to earthquakes.

By the time the façade of the cathedral was designed, responsibility for the work had passed to the architect Manuel Guiterrez Sencio. He lightened the imposing bulk of the cathedral with a two-tiered, Baroque central portal executed in dark-red Andean stone. On the whole, Cuzco Cathedral is austere rather than beautiful, with a formal grandeur that is widely admired by critics and art historians. Harold Wethey, an expert on Spanish colonial architecture, has pronounced it the finest church in the Western Hemisphere.

The paintings and statuary inside the cathedral offer a somewhat more intimate view of the mingling of two cultures. Here, among the thoroughly Spanish carved cedar-wood screens, gilded choir stalls, and jeweled reliquaries, stands the work of Incan artists who interpreted Christian symbols in the light of their own experience. An obscure painting, for example, by an Indian artist shows Christ and His disciples sitting down to a Last Supper of roasted guinea pig. More typical are representations of Christ with distinctly Incan features and pictures showing Mary as either an Incan noblewoman or a bejeweled Spanish aristocrat.

Ironically, Cuzco Cathedral is not rich in gold. It boasts, however, a few objects made from precious metals, such as a silver-plated altar and a famous gold-work monstrance said to contain a thorn from Christ's crown. The greatest part of the treasure of Cuzco made its way to Europe never to return. It is difficult to say who ultimately benefited from this theft. Most of the original members of Pizarro's band either died in the New World or gambled away their share of the booty. Spain became the richest country in Europe, but the sudden influx of gold eventually precipitated a disastrous economic depression. And the Incas, who never used gold as money and would have gladly exchanged all they possessed for their ruler's life, saw their young civilization utterly destroyed.

In the long run, the mingling of the Spanish and Indian cultures had produced a unique Latin American identity. But the Quechua-speaking Indians of the high mountains never really recovered from the loss of Cuzco. Today, one often sees Indian beggars in the Plaza del Armas, a condition that would not have existed under Incan rule. Cuzco Cathedral is an architectural triumph, yet to twentieth-century eyes, it is primarily a tragic symbol of the era when the cross of the conquistadors was first raised over the fallen temples of the ancient pagan gods.

Angkor Wat

Cambodia

Preceding page, the Hindu temple of Angkor Wat, proclaimed to be the divine embodiment of its builder Suryavarman II (1113–1150), Cambodia's "Sun King." This monumental example of classical Khmer art is shown here as it appeared before the Angkor province fell to the Red Khmers in 1971. The present condition of the complex is not known for certain, though it appears to have survived the war basically intact. During the time the temple was occupied by Communist troops, efforts were made to avoid harming the temple, which served as a radio communications center.

The elaborately carved and ornamented sandstone surfaces of Angkor Wat's towers and their staircases (these pages) are now considerably eroded. They were originally accentuated by touches of gilt and brightly colored paints.

The towers of Angkor Wat (above left) represent the five peaks of Mount Meru, the mythical home of the Hindu gods. The central tower with its porticoed entrance (left) is 229 feet high and faces west, toward the traditional abode of the dead. When French archaeologists entered the tower's sanctuary for the first time in the mid-nineteenth century, they found only a few fragments from a demolished idol, which most probably depicted King Suryavarman as an incarnation of the god Vishnu. Angkor Wat is thought to have been a funerary temple, built to house the king's cremated remains after his death. More important, however, it was the spiritual home of the king's soul during his lifetime—the symbol of his ability to communicate as an equal with the gods on Mount Meru.

The three terraced levels of the base of Angkor Wat are a highly refined adaptation of the elementary step pyramid used in more ancient Khmer temples. The middle gallery (above) is enclosed from the outside while the lower gallery (below) opens outward—a reversal of the more familiar cloister form found in Christian church architecture.

During the Angkor period, stone buildings were reserved for the use of the gods. Khmer architects excelled in decoration and sculpture and employed sophisticated tricks of perspective. However, their technical vocabulary was limited by their lack of experience with stone construction. The simple corbelled vault of the outermost gate house gallery (near right) is typical. This outer gallery is connected to the lowest terrace of the central part of the temple by a cross-shaped arrangement of open galleries (far right, above and below), which form four smaller rectangular courtyards.

French archaeologists, whose reconstruction work at Angkor Wat was completed in 1953, were sometimes criticized for destroying the temple's romantic aura when they stripped away the jungle vegetation. Their work, however, made it possible to appreciate the symbolic form of the temple's galleries (left) and gateways (below). Unfortunately, the scholars were too late to rescue the serpent-shaped balustrade and stone lion (above). The ornamental columns of the gallery windows (below right) diffuse the tropical sunlight.

Two religions coexisted during much of Angkor Wat's history. In twelfth-century Cambodia, the Buddhists (above far left) were beginning to outnumber the Hindus, whose rich epic tradition is celebrated in this battle scene (above right). The apsaras *(above center, left, and below) were divine dancers who would perform for King Suryavarman in his next life on Mount Meru. These lithesome entertainers were a favorite subject of Angkor Wat sculptors.*

Twentieth-century Cambodian dancers (above) perform in the forecourt on the causeway in front of the temple's western entrance and (below) pose before carved apsaras whose fantastic headdresses were obviously the inspiration for their jeweled tiaras. Such scenes, often enacted for the benefit of tourists during the 1960s, were most likely only a pale reflection of the ceremonies staged here during the twelfth century, when the temple courtyards were hung with rich, hand-colored silk canopies.

Following page, Angkor Wat as it was before Cambodia was once again swallowed by the political turmoil that has plagued the country since the fourteenth century. Constantly threatened with destruction, whether from warfare or simple neglect, Angkor Wat has proved to be as improbably durable as the spirit of Khmer nationalism. Angkor Wat's prospects for survival have become a more urgent enigma than any of the unanswered questions posed by its long history.

Angkor Wat Cambodia

"One of these temples—a rival to that of Solomon and erected by some ancient Michelangelo—might take an honorable place beside our most beautiful buildings. It is grander than anything left to us by Greece or Rome...." These lines were composed by the French naturalist Henri Mouhot, who played a large part in introducing Europe to the glories of the Khmer temples of Angkor. Mouhot traveled in Indochina between 1858 and 1860, and he was enchanted by the discovery of these stone masterpieces standing solitary and mysterious in the green heart of the jungle. Nevertheless, Mouhot prefaced his enthusiastic description with the ominous note that "the present state of Cambodia is deplorable and its future menacing."

Mouhot was not the first to lament the decline of the Khmer nation. As early as 1296, a Chinese diplomat named Chou Ta-kuen visited the court at Angkor and wrote that the countryside had been devastated by "the recent war with Siam," and its wonderful monuments were beginning to show signs of neglect. Chou Ta-kuen's warning was somewhat premature, for the Khmer empire survived another 150 years. By the nineteenth century, however, even the memory of its magnificence was growing vague. Mouhot found Angkor abandoned, its temples overrun by jungle vegetation. When he asked the local peasants about the monuments' history, he was told only that they were the work of the "leper king." This explanation was quickly discounted by the French scholars and archaeologists who followed Mouhot. They established that the temples were the creation of not just one but many kings who reigned over a period of four centuries. Even so, it was some time before these experts could begin to unravel the enigmas posed by the monuments of Angkor.

The influence of Hindu culture is so pervasive in Cambodia that scholars once surmised that the land was populated by migrants who came from India in historical times. In fact, the Khmers of Cambodia are an ancient, indigenous people who have absorbed influences from many quarters without ever losing their ethnic identity. Remote though it may seem from the West, Cambodia has been affected by events in Europe since the first century A.D., when the Roman Empire's growing demand for goods from the Orient—pearls, gold, silk, rhinoceros horn, and above all, exotic spices—sent a flood of Indian merchants into Southeast Asia en route to markets in China, Vietnam, and the East Indies.

Although Khmer culture was profoundly changed by this contact with India, the direct inspiration for the founding of Angkor came from quite another direction—Java. Historians are still debating the nature of the link between Cambodia and the powerful Sailendra dynasty that arose in Java during the eighth century. Some say that the Sailendra kings were descendants of emigrants from the Cambodian kingdom of Funan, which was broken up in the sixth century A.D. Others contend that the Sailendras merely took advantage of the dissolution of Funan to extend their domain into the mainland of Indochina.

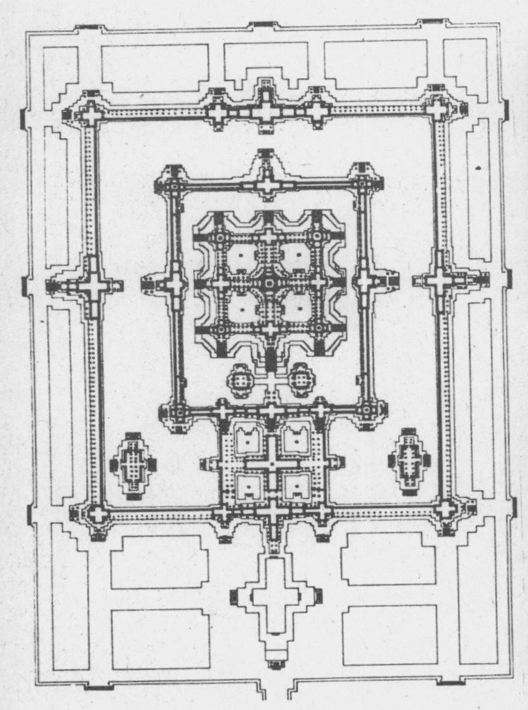

A ground plan (above) and aerial view (right) of Angkor Wat show the five central towers enclosed by the double wall.

Above, a bas-relief of a Teveda, a sacred wife of the god-king. Right, a highly stylized depiction of a Khmer warrior.

Angkor Wat's mile-long gallery of intricately carved reliefs depicting gods, heroes, and dancing girls marked the flowering of classical Khmer art. Immediately above, a scene from the Ramayana epic, dramatizing the death of Hanuman the Monkey King.

In any case, the return to Cambodia in A.D. 790 of a Javanese-educated Khmer prince, Jayavarman II, marked a turning point in the country's history. Through the introduction of a system of large-scale irrigation, Jayavarman II was able to consolidate a number of kingdoms and, eventually, to establish his independence from Java. The center of his irrigation system, and the new capital of Cambodia, was located in the province of Angkor.

As a symbol of his hard-won autonomy, Jayavarman soon adopted the institution of divine kingship practiced by his Javanese mentors, who styled themselves "Kings of the Mountain." This title was a direct reference to an old Hindu tradition which held that the gods resided on mythical Mount Meru. Thus the typical form of the Hindu temples—a stepped pyramid topped by one or more sanctuary towers—was a symbolic representation of this mountain home of the gods. When a king proclaimed himself divine, the temple-mountain became his spiritual home as well. Jayavarman, for example, identified himself with Shiva, who controlled the ebb and flow of life's energies. Hence, the *lingam,* a phallic monument located in the sanctuary of the temple of Shiva, was revered as the resting place of the king's soul.

Jayavarman and his successors did not, of course, live in the temple-mountains they built since the temples were used solely for religious purposes. They may also have served as mortuaries, receiving the cremated remains of the god-kings. While the kings of Angkor were erecting these temples, they and their subjects continued to live in wood palaces and homes clustered around the temples. These wooden structures, however, were long ago destroyed by the humid jungle climate, leaving only the now-solitary Khmer temples as reminders of the time when Angkor Wat was a heavily populated agricultural capital.

The nation founded by Jayavarman II came to full flower in the early twelfth century under the rule of King Suryavarman II, who is sometimes compared to the Sun King, Louis XIV. Although he came to the throne in 1113 as the heir to a relatively new and untried dynasty, Suryavarman lost no time in building a reputation as an energetic military leader and builder. The crowning achievement of this ruler, who awarded himself the title of "protégé of the sun," was the creation of an enormous temple complex, symbolic of his personal unity with the Hindu pantheon. Covering an area of more than 20,000 square feet, Angkor Wat is universally recognized as the gem of classical Khmer art.

The style of Angkor Wat does not represent a new departure. Rather it is an exquisite reinterpretation of an established tradition. The basic form—five towers set atop a three-step base surrounded by a moat—is an elaboration of the temple-mountain theme and recalls a traditional description of Mount Meru as a five-peaked mountain rising directly out of the sea.

The temple's layout, however, demonstrates that the anonymous Khmer architects, though they had limited experience in building with stone, possessed a sophisticated understanding of the rules of perspective. For example, the three tiers of

By the end of the twelfth century, Buddhism had replaced Hinduism as the religion of the Khmer kings. This shift was accompanied by a swing toward more extreme and naturalistic sculpture, as exemplified by the elephant court of the temple of Angkor Thom (left). The meditating Buddha (below) and the so-called "Buddha's Foot," with its inscribed Tao symbols (bottom), have replaced the images of Shiva and Vishnu.

the temple base are scaled to give distant observers the impression that they are of equal height. Further, the length of the great balustraded causeway leading to the western gate is approximately twice the width of the temple base, a proportion calculated to give arriving worshipers the most impressive view of the overall form.

The causeway to Angkor Wat passes over the moat—a 600-foot-wide artificial lake carpeted by fragrant lotus blossoms—and proceeds toward the main gate house, whose façade is a perfect copy in miniature of the temple proper. Gradually, the complexity of the sanctuary is resolved into a recognizable arrangement of two external enclosures with a third inner one, each on a raised terrace. One enters the

inner courtyards of the first level, where decorated galleries—a mile in length—reveal a celestial world populated by Hindu gods and epic heroes. In Suryavarman's day, when these six-foot-high reliefs were accentuated by touches of bright color and the maze of courtyards was hung with canopies of patterned silk, Angkor Wat must have seemed a worthy surrogate for heaven.

Suryavarman's temple-mountain differed from those of his predecessors in one significant respect: The dominant presence at Angkor Wat was no longer Shiva but the god Vishnu, the "world preserver." The twelfth-century Cambodian monarch's decision to identify himself with Vishnu was, in a way, a claim to a more

Below and left, sculpted reliefs of the Banteay Srai Temple erected in A.D. 967. An early use of formal motifs and ritualized postures, these reliefs foreshadow the classical style of Angkor Wat.

exalted divinity and a signal of the approaching extinction of the god-king tradition. In addition to being granted the supreme place in the Mount Meru pantheon by Indochinese Hindus, Vishnu was especially popular with the growing population of Buddhists who believed that the founder of their faith was actually the ninth and last incarnation of this deity. By the reign of Angkor's last notable king, the enigmatic Jayavarman VII, the trend had reached its logical culmination. In the many temples built by Jayavarman, who may indeed have been a "leper king" as the peasant tradition suggests, the image enshrined was neither Shiva nor Vishnu but the king himself as a "Buddha to be."

When this royal "Buddha" died in 1219, the Angkor empire began to disintegrate. Historians have suggested many causes for the decline, from the decentralizing influence of Buddhism to a series of costly border wars. Some even blame the Angkor temples themselves. The construction of so many monumental stone structures may have placed unbearable burdens of taxation and forced labor on the peasantry, leading to domestic rebellion.

For whatever reasons, the irrigation canals of Angkor were no longer maintained after the fifteenth century, and the consequent failure of the rice harvests, as well as epidemics of malaria spawned by the stagnant canal waters, soon emptied the Angkor province. The jungle reclaimed the Khmer temples until 1933, when French archaeologists initiated a major restoration campaign.

Although French colonial domination of Cambodia came on the heels of several centuries of hegemony by Siam and other Indochinese powers, Khmer nationalism was far from defunct. In 1907, the French novelist and travel writer Pierre Loti metaphorically summed up the situation thus: "Despite their much reduced circumstances, the Cambodians have remained Khmers. . . . They have never given up hope of recovering their capital, shrouded for centuries by the Siamese forests."

With the triumph of the Khmer Rouge, the first half of this judgment has been borne out. However, the attitude of today's Khmer leaders toward the temple-mountains is still a mystery. Throughout the Cambodian conflict of the 1970s, there were reports that the temple complex had been shelled and that the Khmers were selling its ancient statuary in Thailand to raise money for munitions. Nevertheless, the Cambodian government requested that all military forces restrict shelling in the vicinity of the temples. It now seems that Angkor Wat may have survived the war in better condition than was once feared. In 1971, the Khmers allowed Cambodian workers wearing blue and white UNESCO armbands to enter the temple with the aim of moving statuary to nearby museums. The Cambodians also buried hundreds of statues that were too large to move. Thanks to their efforts, thousands of bronze and stone works have been preserved for posterity.

The future of Suryavarman's temple-mountain now belongs to the descendants of those anonymous peasants who labored under the autocratic rule of this god-king. Whether they will regard Angkor Wat as a symbol of their ancestors' aspirations or of their oppression remains to be seen.